THE HIBS STORY

An Official History of
Hibernian Football Club

Mike Wilson

g

Grange
Lomond Books

© 1998
Published by Grange Communications Ltd
Edinburgh

Printed in the UK

ISBN 0 947782 16 8

CONTENTS

Acknowledgements

Thanks to Kenny Barclay, Brian Mark, John R Mackay, Tom O'Malley, Rikki Raginia, Lawrie Reilly, Mike Stevenson and Tom Wright for their help.

FOREWORD

HIBERNIAN FC may have been relegated at the end of season 1997/98 to the First Division, but they remain one of Scotland's biggest clubs, a status built on the twin traditions of flair and innovation.

This is the club of the *Famous Five* and *Turnbull's Tornadoes*. This is the first club in Britain to play in European competition, reaching the semi final of the inaugural European Cup in season 1955/56. It is also, remarkably, a club still looking for its first Scottish Cup win since 1902.

This is a deliberately selective slant on the Hibernian's illustrious history.

Whatever their present plight, Hibs are, and will forever be, *Big Time*.

TURNING BACK
THE CLOCK

A REPUTED £5,000 was the price of the newspaper exclusive that greeted Hibs fans on Monday morning, June 4, 1990. The banner headlines had the sobering effect of putting everything else into perspective. Hibs had not lost a league match against supposed underdogs. Nor had they lost yet another Scottish Cup Final. Nor had they been relegated. It was worse than that. They were the subject of so-called 'merger' talks with Edinburgh rivals, Heart of Midlothian. It was called a merger; in reality, it was a takeover attempt.

Leading the charge was Hearts chairman, Wallace Mercer. The logic of his argument was that Edinburgh's two main football clubs would shed the tag of constant under-achievers if they pooled their resources. His route into Hibs was an option to buy shares from Hibs' biggest shareholder, a certain David Rowland.

Rowland was neither Hibs fan nor local boy made good. But he was drawn into Hibs through the club's then chairman, David Duff. To finance the purchase of Hibs from previous chairman, Kenny Waugh, Duff had been bank-rolled by Rowland. The strategy was simple: Duff would launch a share issue in the club to raise capital and - arguably - make the club more accountable to fans; Rowland would be gifted 30 per cent for his trouble. It was that same 30 per cent that Mercer was able to build his bid upon.

Mercer had two targets in mind: 50.1% of the shares would give him control but probably a lot of hassle from disgruntled shareholders continually calling for Extraordinary General Meetings. With 76%, he could do whatever he liked, including asset-strip Hibs and throw away the carcass.

The race was on to prevent any further shares - especially those owned by financial institutions, who would, naturally, be less persuaded by sentiment - falling into Mercer's hands.

Hibs fans rallied to the cause as never before. Sacrifices were commonplace. An abundance of skills was made freely available. There were dozens - hundreds, even - of unsung heroes, contributing whatever services, money and ideas they could.

A 'Hands off Hibs' committee - centred on the Hibernian Supporters' Association - was quickly formed, led by Kenny McLean Snr, a former director.

A rally arranged for Easter Road the following weekend by the Hibs fanzine, *The Proclaimer*, quickly came under the 'Hands off Hibs' umbrella. Before the bid, the fanzine had been warning, for some time, of the vulnerability of the share structure.

Over 6,000 fans attended the rally. The local authority - in the shape of, ironically, Hearts fan, councillor Steve Cardownie - pledged its support. Hibs legends Pat Stanton and Joe Baker received the adulation of the crowd, with Baker sending the place wild when he kissed the Easter Road turf. Ewan Stewart, the chairman of the Hibernian Shareholders' Association, was a key figure, as were the pop group, T*he Proclaimers*, who performed a heart-rending version of 'You'll Never Walk Alone'.

Hibs were front page news for the best part of six weeks. The campaign was a huge undertaking that operated with only a few internal tensions.

The 'Hands off Hibs' committee met almost daily, dreaming up all sort of tactics. At the club, there were separate initiatives to recruit a 'white knight' to save the day. The public side to the campaign attracted a lot of media attention. There were individual stunts, such as a protest outside the headquarters of the Bank of Scotland in the hope it would resist throwing its financial weight behind the bid. Television presenter, John Leslie, sported a Hibs strip emblazoned with 'Hands off Hibs', on the children's programme, 'Blue Peter'.

Letters of support poured in from all corners of the country, including from many Hearts fans. There were behind-the-scenes discussions to guarantee that, even if the worst came to the worst, there would still be a *Hibernian* playing football. Contingencies were explored to ensure that the club's memorabilia and place in the Scottish League could be hived off so that, even if meant playing in the lowest division in the League, at Edinburgh's municipal stadium, Meadowbank, and using a team of hastily-recruited amateurs, there would still be a team for Hibs fans to support.

There was even an informal discussion about the chances of recruiting players from the Ukrainian football club, Dynamo Kiev, given a twinning arrangement that existed between Edinburgh and Kiev.

David Duff's position soon became vital to Hibs' very survival. Were he to succumb to the temptation of selling-out to Mercer (and, later, he was to claim that the figure of one million pounds was dangled in front of him), then Hibs would be done.

In the heat of the moment, some people found it difficult to forgive him for taking the club to the brink in the first place. In the end, he ignored the occasional verbal assaults and remained loyal. A sense of honour prevailed in the club's darkest hour.

Come Friday, July 13, it was all over. Mercer backed down. The emotional argument had triumphed.

It didn't quite mean Hibs were completely out of the woods. A subsidiary leisure group was under-performing and though Hibs had escaped a takeover bid, its accounts remained in poor condition.

Soon enough, Hibs would fall into receivership, to be salvaged by one of Scotland's highest-profile entrepreneurs, Tom, now Sir Tom, Farmer. But at least it was safe from extinction.

Hibernian are alive and kicking, even if there are reasons to be less than cheerful in 1998.

But 1990 was not the first time Hibs had had to bounce back from adversity. Not long after its founding in 1875, Hibs actually went out of existence for a short while. But after having seemingly played its last game in February 1891, the club was resurrected the following year by a group of fans which included a certain Philip Farmer, the great, grand-uncle of Sir Tom.

At the time, perhaps the world needed twice reminding about the mighty Hibernian. Already, the club had won the Scottish Cup - in 1887, thanks to a 2-1 win over Dumbarton. It had even enjoyed the distinction of being crowned 'World Club Champions', after defeating Preston North End in a challenge match in the same year.

But these were turbulent times in Scottish football, as clubs formed and folded on a regular basis. The demise of Hibs was a case in point. Despite appearing to be one of the bigger clubs in Scotland, it was plunged into crisis after a mass exodus of its players to the newly-created Celtic.

Like Celtic, Hibs were a Victorian exercise in self-improvement, with roots firmly established in the Irish immigrant community.

With the blessing of Canon Edward Hannon, the club was formed by members of the Catholic Young Men's Society attached to the St Patrick's Church in the Cowgate area of Edinburgh (back then, an enclave of Irish immigrants). Its first captain was Michael Whelahan.

And up to its demise in 1891, Hibs were a 'Catholics-only' club, prompting resentment in some quarters of the football establishment of the time. Its acceptance into the Scottish Football Association was less than smooth and, in 1887, it was almost stripped of its Scottish Cup win, on the relatively flimsy pretext that a player, Willie Groves, had been paid money - in contravention of the amateur code that persisted at the time.

Indeed, even after the club had reformed under non-sectarian lines, there were pockets of suspicion that meant, for example, that, despite finishing top of Division Two at the end of season 1893/94, the club was refused promotion to Division One.

Finishing top of Division Two at the end of the following season proved irresistible, however. Throughout its history, Hibernian have been out of the highest division in the land just three times - at the end of seasons 1930/31, 1979/80 and 1997/98.

The lean times must be set against the great. For instance, the Scottish Cup and Championship-winning sides at the turn of the century. A 1-0 win over Celtic in the Scottish Cup Final of 1902 was followed, the next season, by the first of Hibs' four

Championship wins.

There have also been two eras so rich in flair and achievement that they are known simply by the shorthand, *Famous Five* and *Turnbull's Tornadoes*.

The *Famous Five* - arguably the best forward line in the history of the domestic game - were an early 1950s phenomenon. *Turnbull's Tornadoes* came along in the early 1970s. Each time, there was success a-plenty (except, incredibly, in the Scottish Cup).

Hibs have also long enjoyed the reputation of being innovators. They were the first British club to play in European competition (the inaugural European Cup of season 1955/56). In the 1980s, they broke the mould by allowing shirt sponsorship. They have also led the way in stadium improvements, being among the first clubs to embrace, firstly, floodlighting, then, later, undersoil heating.

Typical of the volatility of the early years, Hibs played at a variety of locations before settling down at Easter Road. At first, like many football clubs in Edinburgh, Hibs played at The Meadows parkland in the south of the city. Thereafter, they played at such places as Powderhall, Mayfield and even a site little more than a quarter of a mile south of the present ground.

Also typical of these early years, is doubt as to who became the club's first manager. The problem is essentially one of definition. It is not as if the manager's role is tightly defined even to this day, what with the emergence of the 'general manager' to oversee transfer and salary negotiations.

By common consent, the first Hibs manager who was mostly, if not exclusively, involved in coaching and selecting the team was Davy Gordon. But that is not to say some Hibs historians hold differing opinions. It depends on whether the secretary was effectively the manager and also the extent to which the team was picked by committee.

Arguably, from 1875 to 1891, the 'manager' was Canon Hannan. Then, from 1893 to 1919, Dan McMichael (who died in the flu epidemic of 1919). Then, Davy Gordon, from 1919 to 1921.

As the definition settles, so identification becomes clearer: Alex Maley (1921-25), Bobby Templeton (1925-35), Johnny Halligan (caretaker, 1935), Willie McCartney (1935-48), Hugh Shaw (1948-61), Walter Galbraith (1961-64), Jock Stein (1964-65), Bob Shankly (1965-69), Willie McFarlane (1969-70), Dave Ewing (1970-71), Eddie Turnbull (1971-80), Willie Ormond (1980), Bertie Auld (1980-82), Pat Stanton (1982-84), John Blackley (1984-86), Alex Miller (1986-96), Jocky Scott (caretaker, 1996), Jim Duffy (1996-98) and Alex McLeish (1998-present day).

What makes the takeover bid of 1990 pleasantly ironic is that, from the depths of adversity, Hibs returned with the bit between their teeth, winning the Skol League Cup in the autumn of 1991.

What chance Hibs will bounce back from relegation to the First Division at the end of season 1997/98 with victory in the competition which proved so elusive for so many great Hibs managers, the Scottish Cup?

EUROPEAN NIGHTS

WITH THE last two summer tours having been within the United Kingdom, Hibernian don't even have the fallback of pre-season training as a way of treading foreign soil. But that's not to say the great nights of European football are a dim and distant memory. Twice, they have reached the semi final of European competition and some of the great clubs of Europe have played under the Easter Road floodlights. And of all Scottish clubs, Hibernian were the first to explore the potential of playing on such a prestigious stage.

The club's tour of Brazil in 1953 and the far-sightedness of the chairperson, Harry Swan, not to mention the exploits of the *Famous Five* forward line, had marked Hibs as one of the most progressive of clubs throughout the UK.

The first European Cup competition was by invitation only. Hibernian were invited. They were among some illustrious company, including Real Madrid, Sporting Lisbon, Partizan Belgrade, Anderlecht, Rapid Vienna, PSV Eindhoven and AC Milan. Less well known nowadays, perhaps, but also involved were Rheims (France), Rot Weiss Essen (West Germany), Djurgaardens (Sweden), Aarhus (Denmark), Voros Lobogo (Hungary), Servette (Switzerland), Gwardia Warsaw (Poland) and Saarbrucken (Saar). Invitations to Chelsea, Holland Sport (Holland), Malmo (Sweden), Moscow Dynamo (USSR) and Sparta Prague (Czechoslovakia) were, for various reasons, turned down.

It was season 1955/56. Even though the best days of the *Famous Five* were behind them, they still, from that impressive list, made it to the semi final. It doesn't bear thinking about what might have happened had the tournament been inaugurated a couple or so seasons earlier.

The first round saw Hibs paired against the Germans, Rot Weiss Essen, 'Rot Weiss' simply meaning 'Red White'. Aggregate score 5-1, after a 4-0 win in West Germany and a 1-1 draw at Easter Road. The 'away' leg drew a huge Hibs support, thanks to the British Army stationed on the Rhine. Being first on the scoresheet, Eddie Turnbull became the first Briton to score in European club competition. Unlike the appetite for European competition nowadays, the game attracted minimal coverage in the media.

Round two pitched Hibs against Djurgaarden. The odd thing was that, because the Swedish domestic season had yet to wake up from its winter shutdown, the 'away' tie was played at Partick Thistle's ground, Firhill, thus making Hibernian the first Scottish club to have played a European tie in Glasgow. Aggregate score 4-1, after a 3-1 win in Glasgow and a 1-0 win in Edinburgh.

Then came the semi final. It was a game where Hibs' own legends, such as Gordon Smith, met their match in Raymond Kopa. He inspired Rheims to a first-leg 2-0 win at the Parc de Princes in Paris. The return leg at Easter Road resulted in another win for

Rheims, this time 1-0. Though Hibs battled hard in the return, it was to no avail. In both legs, Rheims played a typically continental game of containment and counter-attack. In the match at Easter Road, a late breakaway sealed the tie and the game finished with Rheims winning 3-0 on aggregate (they then went on to lose 4-3 in the final against Real Madrid).

The Hibs team that April 15 evening at Easter Road was Tommy Younger, Willie McFarlane (later, Hibs manager), John Paterson (father of Craig, who was to play for Hibs), John Buchanan, John Grant, Bobby Combe, Gordon Smith, Eddie Turnbull (later, Hibs manager), Lawrie Reilly, Jimmy Thomson and Willie Ormond (later, Hibs manager). The only member of the *Famous Five* not to feature was Bobby Johnstone, who had already left the club for Manchester City.

Once bitten by the bug, Hibs would never again be twice shy. For wonderful memories, Hibs need look no further than the UEFA Cup, which was originally called the Inter Cities Fairs Cup to be competed for by cities rather than individual clubs (which is why the first final, in 1958, saw Barcelona defeat London 8-2 on aggregate).

Hibernian have played 60 ties in the Fairs/UEFA Cup, with one of the great nights being against Barcelona themselves. It was season 1960/1961. A 4-1 aggregate win in the final of the previous season's competition (over Birmingham) meant that Barcelona were drawn against Hibernian in the second round of the competition as defending champions. Hibs had sailed through the first round, on a 'walkover', after Swiss side, Lausanne, scratched from the competition.

At the time, the Fairs Cup was organised outwith UEFA and because of that, Barcelona had the double distinction of also taking part in the European Cup that season. Furthermore, they had the treble distinction of being the first side in six years to knock out the mighty Real Madrid in that competition.

The first leg was in Spain. In the Nou Camp stadium, Hibs came away with a 4-4 draw. It was a shock result that would have been even more staggering had they held on to the 2-0 then 4-2 lead they carved with goals from Joe Baker, Tommy Preston (twice) and Johnny McLeod. But with less than a quarter of an hour to go, Barcelona found enough in reserve to claw back and level the scores. From an 'away goals' point of view, it didn't matter that Hibs had scored four, for the simple reason that the 'away goals' rule was not yet in operation.

But the return at least saw Hibernian on their own patch and with the famous Easter Road slope as the trump card up their sleeve. Hibs lined up: Ronnie Simpson, John Fraser, Joe McClelland, John Baxter, Jim Easton, Sammy Baird, John McLeod, Tommy Preston, Joe Baker, Bobby Kinloch and Willie Ormond. The date was February 23, 1961.

Hibs v Barcelona at Easter Road.

Baker recollects the crowds converging on Easter Road. After having done a day's work (he was an apprentice engineer during his early days at Hibs), he took a train from Shotts to the west end of Edinburgh's main thoroughfare, Princes Street, thus leaving a near two-mile walk to Easter Road because there were no taxis to be found and public transport was mobbed with supporters.

In his overalls and with his haversack on his back, he finally made it to the dressing room at seven o'clock, just 30 minutes before kick-off. Much to the relief of an exasperated manager.

Defying the bookies' pessimistic odds of 7-2 against, Hibs made a whirlwind start, with McLeod and Baker both going close before Baker was, for the third time in as many minutes, fouled on the edge of the penalty box. With just ten minutes on the clock, McLeod flighted in the cross and Baker bulleted a header into the net.

The goal stung the Catalonians into action. An effort by Luis Suarez hit the woodwork before Martinez struck the equaliser on the half-hour mark.

Fourteen minutes later, on the verge of half-time, Barcelona were in the lead, thanks to Hungarian, Sandor Kocsis. Half-time score: Hibernian 1 Barcelona 2.

The task facing Hibs was plain for all to see. But shooting down the slope, they went chasing goals. Three times there were appeals for penalties as Baker (twice) and Kinloch were fouled and three times they were turned down in favour of indirect free-kicks.

The action hots up against Barcelona.

With sixteen minutes remaining and with the scoreline still at 2-1 for the visitors, the odds seemed stacked against Hibs. With the pressure becoming unbearable, Ormond knocked a corner into the box, for Baird to head across goal, where Preston was on hand to head home.

Two apiece and bedlam. Barcelona were conceding free-kicks almost non-stop. The clock ticked down. Then, with five minutes to go, Baker sent a ball into the box for McLeod to run on to. Just as the shot was about to be unleashed, Barcelona fullback, Garay, commited a foul. Penalty!

Immediately, the Barcelona players surrounded the referee, Malka, in protest. The incident was prolonged and unsavoury. European 'Player of the Year', Suarez, was seen to kick the referee. The flare-up threatened to overshadow the drama of the game itself. And, meanwhile, Bobby Kinloch had to stay focused to take the penalty kick. When, eventually, he did, he coolly sent the ball into the back of the net.

By this time, the police were having to intervene to restore calm. When the final whistle went to register an historic victory for Hibs (3-2 on the night, 7-6 on aggregate), the referee was already hovering by the tunnel to make a quick getaway under police protection. A few minutes later, to paraphrase the well-known tongue-twister, the Leith police were forced to 'dismisseth' Barcelona players from kicking in the door to the referee's room.

The win took Hibs into the semi final. They were paired against AS Roma. The first game was at Easter Road and ended in a 2-2 draw, with Joe Baker and John McLeod the

Hibs' scorers.

In the return, manager Hugh Shaw pulled off a masterstroke by bluffing the Italians into believing the player in the No.9 shirt was Baker, whose scoring exploits were bound to attract some physical attention. Instead of Baker, Kinloch wore the No.9 jersey and, as predicted, was heavily marked. Baker, meanwhile, wearing the No.8 shirt, scored twice.

2-2 at Easter Road; 3-3 in Rome. Since the 'penalty shoot-out' was not yet part of the European scene, the tie had to be decided by a third game, a play-off. Just why Hibs conceded to the decider being played in Rome during the Scottish close season is open to speculation. Certainly, the venue was exchanged for a fat cheque.

But, just one game away from the final, a rusty-looking Hibs side capitulated 6-0, their worst-ever defeat in European competition. Roma went on to defeat Birmingham 4-2 in the final.

Consolation came with another run in the Fairs Cup the following season, though it ended in the second round at the hands of a classy Red Star Belgrade, who won 4-0 at home and 1-0 in Scotland.

The next major milestone in Hibs' European history did not occur for a few seasons, again in the Fairs Cup, this time against Napoli of Italy. But that's not to say the intervening years were without incident. Hibs still continued to grace the European stage, playing, for example, Spanish side, Valencia, in successive seasons, losing both times, with the second encounter having to go to a play-off (the venue decided in the Spaniards' favour on the toss of a coin) after the scores were locked at 2-2 on aggregate.

There was also an imaginative 'friendly' lined up for Easter Road between Hibs and Real Madrid. Jock Stein was the Hibs manager at the time. The game was played as a foretaste of further European adventures and to test just how ambitious the Hibs board of directors was, especially since Real's appearance fee was £10,000. The board responded positively and the game went ahead on October 7, 1964.

With ticket prices a relatively expensive six shillings, or 30p in today's currency (with no concessions available), it was far from being a full house in Edinburgh, but those who turned up on that rain-soaked evening were treated to some amazing football, including the maturing of a young Hibs player called Peter Cormack.

Though it was not fully recognised at the time, the game acted as a milestone in the managerial career of Stein who, three years later, guided Celtic to victory in the European Cup itself. Hibs essentially played a 4-3-3 system, with the midfield three being Pat Quinn, Willie Hamilton and John Baxter.

The trio represented a big gamble on Stein's part, since both Quinn and Hamilton were 'flair' players and the consensus was that while one such player was acceptable in midfield, two were a luxury that could be ill-afforded. At the back, Pat Stanton slotted in to partner 'Big John' McNamee in the centre. Up front, the main strike force comprised Neil Martin and Jim Scott, with Cormack operating more on the flank.

Hamilton put in a virtuoso performance. Gifted, but wayward off the field, he played under three Hibs managers, Walter Galbraith, who signed him from Hearts, Stein, who managed to inspire great things from him (includinng his only Scotland cap), and Bob Shankly, who soon sold him to Aston Villa, no doubt sad to lose his footballing genius but nevertheless (to borrow a phrase from journalist, the late Stewart Brown) grateful that he could sleep more soundly at night.

Hamilton, Quinn and the gritty John Baxter disconcerted the Real pattern. A lot of the Spaniards' play was thus forced sideways, nullifying the speed expected of Gento. Stanton and McNamee shackled Puskas. Having started out in imperious fashion, Real were shaken when Cormack, connecting with a Martin cross from the left, smashed Hibs into the lead with a 13th-minute volley. By the time Hibs went 2-0 up, with a second-half own goal from Zoco, not only were Real rattled, Hibs were sending a resounding message across the continent.

In Cormack, Hibs had found a player with ice in his blood, never, it seems, over-awed by the big occasion. It was Cormack, for example, who, in a game at Easter Road against Dunfermline, volleyed a kick-out from the Dunfermline goalkeeper, to score from the half-way line. It was Cormack, for example, who, on his debut for Liverpool (arriving at Anfield via Nottingham Forest), opted to defend a corner by heading the ball back towards his goalkeeper in preference to the more conventional route of upfield.

But anyway, fast forward to season 1967/68 and Napoli. It was a second round game. In the first round, Hibs had accounted for Porto in a match of fluctuating fortunes. A 3-0 'home' leg advantage was added to when Joe Davis scores from the penalty spot within five minutes of the return. However, three goals from the Portuguese side ensured an anxious last few minutes as Hibs were forced to defend their 4-3 aggregate lead.

The first leg against Napoli was away from home. Hibs were comprehensively thumped 4-1, Colin Stein providing a late lifeline when the side were trailing 4-0.

No one gave them an earthly in the return. The Italians were, after all a very strong side, boasting the likes of the Italian national keeper, Dino Zoff, and Brazilian winger, Jarbas Faustinho (known as Cane), who had scored a 'hat-trick' in the first leg. Indeed, so confident were Napoli, they arrived in Scotland having allowed Brazilian (later Italian) international, Jose Altafini, to stay at home.

But Hibs manager, Bob Shankly, had other ideas. He had said as much at the post-match conference in Italy. Few believed his prediction that Hibs could turn the tables. On Wednesday, November 29, 1967, that is exactly what they did.

The game exploded into action with a 40-yarder (which was a cross-cum-shot that deceived Zoff) from right-back Bobby Duncan. Further goals eluded Hibs until just before half-time, when Pat Quinn scrambled home a second. At the interval, the aggregate score stood at 4-3 . . . advantage Napoli, but initiative Hibs.

The 26,000 crowd roared Hibs on as they embarked on the second half, once again with the Easter Road slope in their favour. Up popped Peter Cormack, Pat Stanton and Colin Stein to do the needful. It was 5-0 on the night, 6-4 on aggregate . . . and Shankly faced the press with a wry smile.

Hibs were through. Next stop, Leeds United. December 20, 1967 at Elland Road; January 10, 1968 at Easter Road. During their European adventures, Hibs have met Leeds United twice and Liverpool twice. This was the first of Hibs' ties against Leeds. Both legs were shrouded in controversy, with Leeds, managed by Don Revie, as cynical as they were successful.

In the first leg, Colin Stein - who later became the first player to move between two Scottish clubs (Hibs and Rangers) for a £100,000 transfer fee - appeared to have scored for Hibs. The referee even pointed to the centre-circle until Leeds players protested and the decision was reversed.

It meant that, instead of coming away with a 1-1 draw, Hibs were 1-0 first-leg losers. The additional concern for the return leg was that, following fierce tackling that forced Stein to be stretchered from the Elland Road game, Hibs might be without their main striker.

Stein, fortunately recovered in time. On the right flank for Hibs was veteran former Rangers, Everton and Scotland international, Alex Scott. In other circumstances, it might have been the newly-dubbed 'Scottish George Best', Peter Marinello. If the first leg is remembered for questionable refereeing, the second was no better. Referee, Clive Thomas, invoked the little-used rule that limited goalkeepers to taking four steps when they had the ball in their hands. Hibs goalkeeper, Willie Wilson, was the unfortunate victim of the referee's pedantry. The resulting free-kick was floated in and Jack Charlton, hovering at the far post, headed to score. The game ended 1-1 (Stein being Hibs scorer) and therefore 2-1 in favour of the English side.

The second Hibs-Leeds encounter took place during the 1973/74 season, this time in the UEFA Cup, and again ending in disappointment. The first leg, on October 24, 1973, was at Elland Road. Hibs were dominant, with Bobby Smith and Arthur Duncan tearing Leeds apart on the wing and Tony Higgins preventing the home side's marauding midfielder, Billy Bremner, from exerting any influence.

The game ended 0-0. It might have been 1-0 for Hibs, but an unfortunate Higgins, no doubt brimming with confidence, decided to step in ahead of team-mate and proven goalscorer, Alan Gordon, to head a great opportunity over the crossbar.

Having totally out-played Leeds in Leeds and, as far as Hibs manager, Eddie

Turnbull, was concerned, beat Revie at his own game, expectations were high for the return on November 7.

Leeds' response was to push Bremner into the role of sweeper and counter Higgins with Norman 'Bite Yer Legs' Hunter. Hibs, nevertheless, played some sparkling stuff, forcing Bremner to have one of the games of his life. After 90 minutes it was 0-0. It stayed the same after extra time. 'Penalty shoot-out'. Pat Stanton stepped up to take the first. The shot hit the post. It was to be a crucial miss. With the remaining penalties converted on both sides, Hibs were out 4-5 on penalties after two 0-0 draws.

A somewhat pathetic attempt to have Leeds thrown out of the competition, because their manager and back-room staff contravened rules about who could stand on the pitch during the 'penalty shoot-out', meant that Hibs' name was included in the draw for the next round pending a decision by the authorities. Unsurprisingly, Leeds survived the protest with a small fine.

What to say about the games against Liverpool? There was surely controversy, but, unlike the games against Leeds, they were more of Hibs' own making. The first match was in season 1970/71 (Fairs Cup); the second in 1975/76 (UEFA Cup).

The first leg of the first encounter was played at Easter Road on December 9, 1970. It was preceded, just hours before, by the departure of manager, Willie McFarlane, following a dispute with club owner, Tom Hart, about players. Understandably shaken, the Hibs team were a shadow of themselves, with winger Eric Stevenson trying manfully to adapt to his sudden redeployment as the side's main striker. After losing 1-0 at home, the best Hibs could do on the return at Anfield was lose by a further two goals. Aggregate score: Liverpool 3 Hibernian 0.

Five years later, the clubs were drawn against each other again, this time in the UEFA Cup. The first leg was encouraging. A Joe Harper volley capped fine performances from the likes of Iain Munro and Arthur Duncan. It could have been even better, had John Brownlie converted a last-minute penalty to make it 2-0.

But, still, 1-0 was not an impossible lead to defend.

The problem was an internal fall-out between manager Turnbull and Stanton. In between the first-leg win on September 17 and the return on the 30th, Hibs had lost to Montrose in the League Cup. The giant-killing feat rebounded on Stanton, who was made a scapegoat. Dropped for the return against Liverpool, his absence meant that Hibs had no-one to challenge the home side's striker, John Toshack, in the air. Toshack profited with a 'hat-trick' of headed goals and, though Hibs had gone into the interval at one apiece, following a rasping cross-goal shot from Alex Edwards, the writing was on the wall. On the night, it ended Liverpool 3 Hibernian 1, aggregate 3-2 for the Merseysiders.

While Fairs/UEFA Cup glories abound, Hibs' debut in the Cup-Winners' Cup did not lack excitement, either. The campaign followed Hibs' somewhat inauspicious defeat by Celtic in the previous season's Scottish Cup Final. Despite losing 1-6, Hibernian were the Scottish representatives in the competition because Celtic, as League Champions, were engaged in the European Cup.

If getting into the competition represented a touch of good fortune, Hibs were brought back down to earth with a tough first-round draw, against Sporting Club de Portugal, otherwise known as Sporting Lisbon. Nevertheless, Arthur Duncan's goal in Portugal gave Hibs, wearing all-purple and putting up one of their best-ever displays on foreign soil, a fighting chance for the return at Easter Road.

Trailing 1-2 from the first leg when Sporting scored in as many minutes in the second half, Hibs - this time resplendent in an all-green top - went to work in the second leg.

For ages, however, precious little went to plan. The problem was a very competent Lisbon defence. At half-time, it didn't look particularly encouraging, with the scoreline at 1-1. What happened next was all-too-familiar to Easter Road regulars. Shooting down that famous slope again, Hibs went to town. Jimmy O'Rourke's work that night was finally complete with a 'hat-trick' as Hibs went on to win 6-1 (7-3 on aggregate). The date was September 27, 1972.

This was an era of big scores. On September 20, in the League Cup, Hibs came back from 2-0 down to defeat Dundee United 5-2. In the quarter-final match in the same competition, Hibs were 2-1 down, this time to Airdrie, on October 11, before coming back to win 6-2. In the league, against Ayr United on December 16, a week after having won the League Cup against Celtic, Hibs notched up an 8-1 win. Of course, as every Hibernian fan knows off-by-heart, on January 1, a couple of weeks later, Hibernian put seven goals past their rivals, Heart of Midlothian, again in the league.

Not surprising then, that when Hibs' second-round opponents were a side from the relatively unsophisticated football nation of Albania, another hatful of goals would ensue. The first leg against FC Besa was at home, the Albanians arriving in Edinburgh seemingly more interested in the relative luxury of Scotland than in putting up any sort of resistance on the field. Yet another 'hat-trick' from Jimmy O'Rourke paved the way for an emphatic 7-1 win. The return leg, even though it was a formality, still represented something of an adventure into the unknown. Hibs took everything they needed, including their own food and water. It ended 1-1.

All of Scotland were by now beginning to take an interest in Hibs. *Turnbull's Tornadoes* were beginning to fulfil their potential. They might have lost 1-6 in the previous summer's Scottish Cup Final, but they had since lifted the Drybrough Cup and League Cup and gone to the top of the league following their improbable 7-0 win over Hearts at the start of 1973.

Hibs had a side that were beginning to draw favourable comparisons with the *Famous Five* side of the late 1940s and early 1950s. When the quarter final paired Hibs with Yugoslavian club, Hajduk Split, there were grounds to feel quietly confident. The sense of optimism prevailed over some key setbacks, however, not least the loss of attacking right-back, John Brownlie, whose leg was broken in a game against East Fife just a week after the 7-0 rout of Hearts.

The confidence remained largely intact, even when a very late goal pulled the score back from 4-1 in Hibs' favour to 4-2 in the first leg encounter at Easter Road on March 7, 1973.

But it was all to turn to dust for the return a fortnight later, on March 21. The 3-0 loss (and resulting 4-5 aggregate defeat) seemed utterly in keeping with dipping league form at home, not least because of a lengthy league suspension incurred by Alex Edwards. The defeat in Split was to prove the last Hibs game played by goalkeeper, Jim Herriot, who chose to ignore the advice of his manager, Turnbull, to don some headgear, with the unfortunate result that instead of being plucked out of the air, crosses were being lost in the bright sunshine, and needless goals were being conceded.

It was Turnbull's second full season in charge of Hibs. Since then, the argument has raged whether he was too hasty in making changes to the Hibs team following the Hadjuk Split defeat. But changes he certainly made. He is quoted saying he started losing interest in the side from that point on. "*I lost faith and never regained it,*" he told journalist Simon Pia.

Between 1961 and 1974, some very famous clubs visited Easter Road on European business, including Barcelona, Roma, Hamburg, Porto, Leeds, Napoli, Liverpool, Valencia (twice) and Juventus. And yet only two, Juventus and Liverpool left with a victory over the 90 minutes.

The Juventus defeat (4-2) on October 23, 1974, came in the middle of a particularly bleak week for Hibs on both the European and domestic fronts. At the start of the week, ahead of the game against Juventus, Hibs lost 5-0 in the league to Celtic. At the tail-end of the week, they lost 6-3 in the League Cup Final, again to Celtic.

The second leg of the Juventus game might have yielded a more encouraging result had Stanton converted any of two clear runs on goal within the first quarter of an hour. In the end, a 4-0 defeat ensued, that name from the past, Altafini, from the days of Hibs v Napoli, playing the role of 'supersub'.

It is worth pausing for a moment to consider the Juventus line-up and the galaxy of internationals it contained, including Dino Zoff (another veteran of the Hibs-Napoli contest), Claudio Gentile, Roberto Bettega and Franco Causio. Also playing were

Antonello Cuccureddu and Pietro Anastasi, at the time the world's most expensive player (bought for £440,000, or 666 million lire).

When only 12,000 fans turned up at Easter Road in September 1976 to witness Hibs defeat French side, Sochaux, on the way to a 1-0 aggregate win over the two legs, it seemed entirely in keeping with the mood of the times that their next round opponents should be an unknown side from Sweden called Oesters Vaxjoe. And that, despite a 2-0 advantage from the first leg at home, the Hibs team should, on a pitch that was no more than a mud-bath and in front of a crowd of just 1,715, lose 4-1 to go out 4-3 on aggregate.

For goals, it took another Scandinavian club, Rosenborg Trondheim, in the 1974/75 UEFA Cup to capitulate most to Hibs, losing 9-1 at Easter Road, with Joe Harper (twice), Iain Munro (twice), Alex Cropley (twice), Pat Stanton (twice) and Alan Gordon all getting on the scoresheet.

After a 2-1 aggregate defeat from Racing Strasbourg of France in the UEFA Cup of 1978/79, Hibs left it eleven years before gracing the European stage again. Hungarians, Videoton, were the club's first-round opponents in the 1989/90 UEFA Cup.

With the first leg at home, a looping header from the unlikely source of defender Graham Mitchell, gave Hibs a slender 1-0 advantage. While the return was a step into the unknown, it turned out to be one of the best-ever European nights of them all. Keith Houchen, Gareth Evans and John Collins did the club proud, scoring the goals in a 3-0 win (aggregate score 4-0).

The next round, against FC Liege, was approached optimistically. But for all their efforts, Hibs could not take advantage of playing the first leg at home, Houchen missing a penalty to sharpen the despair. Nevertheless, a large travelling support journeyed to Belgium, again to witness a professional display by Hibs. After 90 minutes, still no goals had been scored. So, on to extra time, resolved, sadly for Hibs, by a long-range effort that slightly deceived goalkeeper, Andy Goram.

At least Hibs fans didn't have to wait another eleven years before returning to the European arena. For winning the Skol Cup against Dunfermline, their reward was a first-round tie against the mighty Anderlecht, also of Belgium. The first leg, at Easter Road, ended 2-2, with Hibs marginally the better of the sides. The return, in the five-star luxury of the Stade Constant Vanden Stock, was again a scoring draw. An estimated 3,000 fans were in Brussels for the game. Darren Jackson was the Hibs scorer. It ended 1-1 (3-3 on aggregate),which meant that Hibs were out on the 'away goals' rule. It was a hard exit to bear.

See Stats at the Back for Hibs' European record.

FAMOUS FIVE

IF THERE is anything that marks Hibernian as a football club of world stature it is that forward line of the late 1940s and early 1950s (reading from right wing to left): Gordon Smith, Bobby Johnstone, Laurie Reilly, Eddie Turnbull and Willie Ormond.

The mathematics of modern football now make it almost impossible to reproduce a forward line in their image. Midfields are permitted to be five-strong, but, further upfield, such adventure is - according to today's thinking - verging on the irresponsible.

Until recently, Blackburn Rovers had a nickname for its forward line. But what chance the 'SAS' of Alan Shearer and Chris Sutton against *The Famous Five*?

They were a line-up ideally suited to their era, when football was enjoying a post-war renaissance unlikely ever to be repeated. Photography was black and white, tracksuits were a heavy cotton, boots were almost hob-nailed, balls were leaden leather and tolerances were such that the quaint cry of *"Gie the ba' tae Reilly"* could rise from the terraces every other Saturday.

Nothing, it seemed, mattered except goals. And all of the *Famous Five* could score. If Hibs lost two, they would score three; if Hibs lost three, they would score four. The *Five's* legacy is that, even to this day, Hibs sides are expected to deliver entertainment first and a result second.

Gordon Smith, the 'Prince of Wingers'; Bobby Johnstone, nippy, unpredictable, an artist with the ball; Lawrie Reilly, goalscorer supreme, for club and country; Eddie Turnbull, the grafter with a thunderbolt shot; Willie Ormond, fast, direct and lethal with the left foot.

But for Johnstone taking his dandy good looks to Manchester City in 1955 in a hasty, £25,000 transfer, all stayed at Easter Road until almost the end of their careers.

That said, Smith managed to eke out five more years in the game than Hibs expected after letting him go in 1959. Spells with Hearts, Dundee, Morton and Irish club, Drumcondra, meant that, come his actual retirement - a month short of his 40th birthday - he had amassed three Championship medals with three different clubs (Hibs, Hearts and Dundee) and appeared in two European Cup semi finals (with Hibs and Dundee). Arguably, he is the only player in the world to have represented three different clubs in the European Cup, now known as the *Champions' League*. Hibs had cut their ties because they didn't expect him to recover properly from ankle surgery.

The Hibs support have, however, never let him leave their affections. Such was his genius with a ball, he could play 'keepie-uppy' along the length of the touchline before scoring with blistering precision. As the line goes: *"Johnstone was braw, Reilly an' 'aw, but the cocky wee Gordon was the pride of them 'aw."*

He was as good as the fabulous Sir Stanley Matthews; better, say many. And yet the 'Gay Gordon' didn't win too many caps - just 18 - thanks, mainly, to Rangers' Willie Waddell, who pressed Smith for the berth on the right wing.

In a patchy sequence of internationals, his best years were, arguably, towards the end of his Scotland career, his last game being against Spain in May, 1957, where he scored the only goal in a 4-1 defeat.

Smith began as a centre-forward before drifting out to the right. During the war, he made 139 league appearances, scoring 96 times. After the war, he made a further 314 league appearances, scoring 127 times.

By 1950, he had been Hibs' top scorer for seven out of eight seasons. His last game for Hibs was in season 1958/59, by which time Joe Baker was already beginning to clatter in the goals (the next season, he scored 42, making him the top scorer in a single season).

1951/52 League Championship-winning side, including the 'Famous Five' sitting in the front row.

But it is against Smith's long Hibs career, lasting 17 years, that the romance conjured by the *Famous Five* must be set.

The fact is, the *Famous Five* played together for just six years. Between the war and the late 1950s, while the club competed in two Scottish Cup Finals and one League Cup Final, the only time all five played in the final of any tournament was in May, 1953, when Hibs lost 2-0 to Celtic in the final of the Coronation Cup, celebrating the crowning of

Queen Elizabeth II.

Being the spiritual godfather of the *Famous Five*, it is appropriate that Gordon Smith should be the first to sign up to the cause. And he marked his entrance with characteristic elan, scoring a 'hat-trick' on his debut on April 30, 1941 against, of all teams, rivals Heart of Midlothian. Being a war-time fixture, the game was played under the auspices of the Southern League. Also being war-time, he learned his trade alongside some notable guests, including Matt Busby, who was to go on to become the legendary manager of Manchester United.

Nevertheless, it wasn't plain sailing for him straight from the start. An early disappointment was being overlooked in favour of the recently-signed international, Jimmy Caskie, from Everton, for the 3-2 Summer Cup win over Rangers in 1941.

However, it wasn't too long before he was able to put that disappointment behind him, scoring twice in another eventful match, a breathtaking 8-1 Southern League win over Rangers in September, 1941.

In a career of such longevity, highlights are thick on the ground. In the third round of the Scottish Cup in February, 1948, for example, Smith masterminded a 4-2 win over Aberdeen, despite the team being reduced by injury to nine players (substitutions weren't allowed at the time).

The previous November (November 8), he slotted five goals in an 8-0 rout of Third Lanark.

And he scored once in his own testimonial match against Manchester United, in September 1952, a 7-3 win for Hibs which has gone down as one of the all-time great games in the club's illustrious history. The testimonial was staged to commemorate Smith making over 500 appearances for Hibs (in all games, including Second XI Cup ties, war-time Summer Cup matches, 'friendlies', continental tours and local cup ties such as the East of Scotland Shield).

As with his *Famous Five* colleagues, Smith was signed by Hibs charismatic manager, Willie McCartney, a man never short of a carnation in the buttonhole of his double-breasted suit jacket. Like the signing of Reilly a few years later, the transaction was completed under the noses of Hearts, who had been credited with an interest in Smith after he had appeared for a Junior XI side playing a Hibs-Hearts Select to mark the opening of a football park in Dundee.

The signing of Reilly did, however, enjoy the advantage that the striker was already a committed Hibs fan, the only one of the *Famous Five* to sign as such.

Reilly made his debut at the tender age of 16, on October 13, 1945, in a Southern League fixture at Kilmarnock. However, he remained a fringe player until 1948. In total, he scored 189 league goals for his one and only club. Sadly, at the equally tender age of 29, a game against Rangers - in which, true to form, he scored in a 3-1 win - was to prove his last.

When injury and injured pride allowed, he was consistently Hibs' top marksman. A bout of pleurisy sidelined him for a few months in 1954. And, after Hibs had refused to grant him a testimonial (a decision later reversed), he protested by spending a few more months out of the game. But that last game, against Rangers, contained all the pathos football can muster.

It was a week before the 1958 Scottish Cup Final, in which Hibs were due to meet Clyde. The matchday programme of April 21 wrote, *"Tonight, Lawrie Reilly says farewell. A fleeting 90 minutes tonight and he will become a Hibernian stalwart of the past."* The reason for such

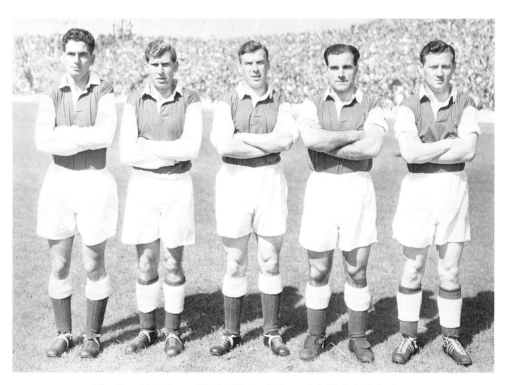

The alternative 'Famous Five', with Combe (second right) in for Johnstone.

pre-meditated departure? Medical advice warned of escalating cartilage problems with his knee, since proved correct.

He scored an incredible number of goals for Hibs. Between season 1950/51 and 1956/57, he was Hibs' top scorer, scoring 23, 27, 30, 15, 15, 23 and 16 league goals. He was not far short of emulating Smith in making 500 appearances for Hibs.

And for Scotland, for whom he made 38 appearances (making him Hibs' most-capped player), he scored 22 goals, a strike rate of 0.58 that eclipses Denis Law (0.55 = 30 goals from 55 appearances) and Kenny Dalglish (0.29 = 30 goals from 102 appearances).

For Scotland, he proved something of a good luck charm, scoring five times in five appearances against England at Wembley. It was after the 1953 Wembley international that he earned the nickname, 'Last Minute Reilly'. England were leading 2-0 going into the last stretch, but Reilly - typically whole-hearted - scored twice to tie the game, the second goal coming in the last minute. His characteristically straightforward response

Lawrie Reilly.

to the nickname is that all games are there to be played all the way to the final whistle, an attitude which contrasted with that of his main rival to the Scotland No.9 shirt, Hearts' Willie Bauld, who was a more laid-back player.

Injury, illness and arrogance denied him the World Cup stage he surely deserved. By the time of the 1958 World Cup in Sweden, he was retired from the game. In 1954 - in Switzerland - he was out because of the pleurisy. In 1950, Scottish arrogance meant that, although there were two places available for British teams at the Brazil World Cup, Scotland declined to participate because they hadn't finished that season's series of games against the other home countries as champions.

Remarkably, Reilly's first dozen international appearances each ended in victory. His international debut was, surprisingly not a scoring one, in a 3-1 win over Wales in Cardiff on October 23, 1948. Twice that year, the Scotland team contained five Hibernian players, in matches against Belgium (at Hampden Park, April 28, 2-0) and Switzerland (in Berne, May 17, 1-2): Jock Govan, Davie Shaw, Gordon Smith, Bobby Combe and Eddie Turnbull, with Combe scoring against Belgium.

But Reilly did score in his next international, a 3-1 win over England at Wembley in April the following year. Throughout, he didn't go more than four internationals without scoring.

Reilly has been quoted as saying the *Famous Five* could have been as easily christened the *Famous Four*, arguing all he did was add the finishing touches to the good work of the other four players, whose success owed much to their ability to play in each other's positions. He is being modest, of course.

But while there is no case to reduce the *Five* to *Four*, there is one to increase it to *Six*. Bobby Combe, who made his Hibs debut in the same game as Gordon Smith and who scored four in the 8-1 win over Rangers in 1941, won three caps for Scotland in April and May, 1948. Perhaps he was a casualty of *The Famous Five* sounding better than the *Sensational Six*. Before settling down to make the No.6 jersey his own at left-half, he was also probably too versatile a player for his own good, as comfortable at the back as he was up front.

If Smith and Reilly are the most heralded of the *Five*, that is not to deny the place of the other three in the pantheon of legends. Johnstone, playing as inside-forward, was the last of the *Five* to make his Hibs debut. He was the most intricate of players. Two-footed and always aware of where defenders were, he was the genius who was the main supplier to Smith. He made his debut on April 2, 1949, in an 'A' Division game at St Mirren. Though he did return to Hibs for a second, short stint - providing the passes that helped forge striker, Joe Baker's, reputation as a stunning goalscorer - with Smith and Reilly having already departed, there was no chance of a *Return of the Five*.

In England, with Manchester City, he scored 42 league goals in 124 appearances. In the club's FA Cup Final appearances of 1955 and 1956, he scored in both, including the 3-1 win, in 1956, over Birmingham City. He returned to Easter Road for a fee of

£6,000. A year later he was back in England, this time with Oldham.

Eddie Turnbull was later to become as lauded for his managerial skills in the 1970s as he was as a player in the 1950s, assembling a side considered second only to that of the *Famous Five* era. He made his Hibs debut at Easter Road against Third Lanark on November 2, 1946. Like Johnstone, it was an 'A' Division match. And he played his last game against Real Gijon on May 31, 1959, during a four-game tour of Spain.

After his playing days were over, he remained for a couple of years at Easter Road as a trainer (appointed on June 11, 1959, along with training supervisor, Jimmy McColl, and training assistant, Jimmy Cumming). Only after the arrival of Walter Galbraith as manager in November, 1961, did he embark on his own managerial career, beginning as trainer at Queen's Park and peaking spectacularly at Aberdeen as well as Hibs. Unlike Reilly, Turnbull at least featured in the 1958 World Cup finals.

In November 1978, he was appointed by Jock Stein to manage the Scotland under-21 team, his first game in charge being a 5-1 win over Norway at, of all places, Easter Road.

The postscript to that game was that Hibs' signing of one of the Norwegian players, Isak Refvik, sparked an immediate protest from the Department of Employment, which was acutely sensitive to the issue of foreign players - such as Argentinians, Ossie Ardiles and Ricky Villa, who had just joined Spurs after their country's World Cup win - plying their trade in the UK.

The matter - given considerable media coverage - was even discussed in the House of Commons, with various MPs, including Alex Fletcher, Tam Dayell, Bruce Millan (Scottish Secretary of State), Gavin Strang, Denis Howell (Minister of Sport), Malcolm Rifkind and Frank McElhone (Scottish Office under-secretary), all arguing Hibs' case, but unsuccessfully. Refvik was forced home.

It forced Tom Hart, the ambitious Hibs chairperson of the time, to remark: *"Twice, he [Refvik] was stopped at Edinburgh and again at Heathrow on our return from Israel and questioned like a political prisoner or foreign terrorist. His English is not so good that he could appreciate why he was being singled out.*

"The United Kingdom contains many persons from abroad and quite a number do not seek employment. They are content to live off social security.

"Devolution might not be a bad thing if it rids us of the shackles of Whitehall. Some people seem to think the UK begins and ends in London."

Meanwhile, Willie Ormond, after managing St Johnstone, Scotland and Hearts, returned to Easter Road in February, 1980 in a managerial capacity, initially as assistant during the last days of the Turnbull years and then on his own, albeit for a few months, as Hibs began their successful battle to return to the Premier Division from the First.

As a player, he was so one-footed, there was a cartoon strip loosely based on him. But that left-foot of his could be lethal. He is said to have once quipped, *"You wouldn't have heard of Pele if I had a right foot."* His trademark was to push the ball ahead and chase after it, before cutting inside to line up a shot. He was predictable but it didn't stop defenders being run ragged. Sports writer, Ian Wood, says of him: *"He was a fearless wee winger whose legs kept breaking, but who moved at speed and had a left foot like a hammer. The term 'impossible angle' might have been invented with Willie Ormond's shooting in mind."* In total, he broke his leg three times, once against Aberdeen in a Scottish Cup tie. In another Scottish Cup tie - this time against Motherwell - he suffered ruptured ligaments.

Ormond was the only player whose signing involved a transfer fee, not that his move from Stenhousemuir cost much, just £1,200. His Hibs debut was at Queen of the South on December 7, 1946. Scottish football was still some ten years away from re-organising itself into a Division One and a Division Two. Hence, his debut was also an 'A' Division fixture. His final game was in the second of Hibs' three Fairs Cup matches against Roma, finishing 3-3 in the Olympic stadium in Rome, on April 26, 1961. After Easter Road, he played for Falkirk before being appointed assistant trainer there in August, 1962.

At St Johnstone - where a stand at McDiarmid Park is named after him - he led the team to famous European victories in the UEFA Cup against SV Hamburg and Vasas Budapest.

As Scotland manager - appointed in January, 1973 - his record was P38 W18 D8 L12, including an undefeated run during the finals of the 1974 World Cup in West Germany. In 1975, he was awarded an OBE for services to football. He left the Scotland job in 1977, succeeded by Ally MacLeod. He died on May 4, 1984, aged 57.

So what was it about the *Five* that has secured their place in the annals of the game? What was it about them that has led the club - almost half a century on - to name one of its new stands at a redeveloped Easter Road in their honour? Or inspire a branch of the supporters association to call themselves - in a clever play on words - the 'Famous Fife'?

The remarkable thing is that when they made their competitive debut as a quintet, it pretty much went unnoticed. Six months earlier, they had lined up for a 'friendly' against Nithsdale Wanderers, in Sanquhar. That was in April, 1949. Their competitive debut was against Queen of the South on October 15. But the talk in the build-up to that game was all about the halfback line and how it had to be changed as a matter of urgency. The previous week, Hibs had lost, fairly abjectly, to Second Division Dunfermline in the semi final of the League Cup. In response, the entire halfback line of Michael Gallagher, Matthew McNeill and Jimmy Cairns was scrapped and a new one of Bobby Combe, John Paterson and Archie Buchanan put in its place. Combe's move back opened the way for Johnstone and thus, somewhat inadvertently, the *Famous Five* was born.

Hibs' three league titles (1947/48, 1950/51 and 1951/52) are quintessential *Famous Five*. Sadly, McCartney never saw these fruits of his labours, collapsing after a Scottish Cup, first-round win over Albion Rovers on January 24, 1948 and dying soon afterwards. He was succeeded by his assistant, Hugh Shaw, who was to remain manager at Easter Road until 1961.

In the eight seasons separating 1945/46 and 1952/53, Hibs topped the table three times and finished runners-up four times (in 1952/53, losing out on 'goal average' - a third, successive Championship would have been theirs had it been decided on the later system of 'goal difference').

What a contrast with the bleak pre-war days, when the club, with precious little money, was little more than a revolving door of journeymen players. It says something about the confidence coursing through the club during those heady, post-war years, that Hibs boasted the most modern matchday programme in the country, under the editorship of Magnus Williamson. Plans were also drawn up at this time to expand Easter Road to a 98,000 capacity stadium, with a new, covered terracing at the Hawkhill end (today's East Stand) to accommodate 17,200.

The 1947/48 League Championship win didn't really take off for Hibs until January, 1948. A Ne'erday win over Hearts (which put Hibs top and the Tynecastle club bottom of the table) and a win against Rangers on the last day of the month were among the key moments.

Nevertheless, there were occasions of note before. Reporting a 2-0 win for Hibs against Motherwell at Fir Park on November 1, 1947, T*he Evening News* described the first of Gordon Smith's two goals, thus: *"Starting in midfield, he bewildered man after man in a swerving run before finally bursting between the backs to score as he fell headlong. A truly brilliant solo effort, one that bore the stamp of greatness."*

Against Rangers on January 31, in a game being billed as the title decider, it was Johnny Cuthbertson who scored the only goal, in the last minute. The poignancy of the victory was that it was in the immediate wake of McCartney's death. T*he Evening News* report of the game carried the headline, *"Bravo Hibernians, A Gallant Triumph"*.

Then, Scottish football was being carved up between Hibs and Rangers, with Hibs enjoying some famous victories over the Glasgow club, such as in the second round of the Scottish Cup in 1951 when, in front of a 100,000 crowd at Ibrox, Hibs twice came from behind to win 3-2, thanks to a clever free-kick move finished off with an overhead strike from Bobby Johnstone.

Just as the dominance of the 'Old Firm' in today's game is the subject of much soul-searching, the duopoly of Hibs and Rangers was a major concern in post-war Scotland. Though it never actually happened, it was often suggested that Scotland as an international team could do a lot worse than select the 'Iron Curtain' defence of Rangers and the *Famous Five* forward line of Hibs. In fact, the nearest the *Famous Five* ever got to playing the same international was a Scottish League international in 1953, when all bar Turnbull played in a 2-0 win over the League of Ireland (Dundee's Billy Steel keeping Turnbull out).

Come the end of January, 1948, the best possible tribute the players could give to the memory of Willie McCartney was to continue their rich vein of form to make the title secure. This they did, with impressive consistency. From start to finish, their home form was particularly eye-catching, reflected in a doubling of the average 'home' gate from 15,000 to 30,000. Their 15 'home' games in the league saw them win 13 and lose twice. In nine of these 15 games, they kept a clean sheet; in seven, they won by at least four goals, including 8-0 against Third Lanark, 7-0 against Airdrie, 6-0 against Queen of the South and 5-0 against Motherwell and St Mirren. By the end of the season, Hibs had the title sewn up with a two-point gap. Hibs finished on 48 points, having scored 86 goals and conceded 27. Runners-up Rangers, on 46 points, had scored 64 and conceded 28. Third was Partick Thistle. Celtic, at the other end of the table, avoided relegation by just four points.

The title win put an end to the 'Old Firm' monopoly since Motherwell's Championship win in season 1931/32.

While the following season was a disappointment as far as defending the league crown was concerned, with too many points dropped during the opening games, Hibs were now a force to be reckoned with. They finished that title race in third place. Rangers, in winning the league flag, became the first club to win the 'Treble' of Championship, League Cup and Scottish Cup.

Only now did the *Five* come together. And the manner of the second title win, in season 1950/51, was emphatic. Indeed, the title was wrapped up with four games of the campaign remaining, four second-half goals against Clyde at Shawfield capturing the league flag. With wins worth just two points, Hibs finished ten points clear of second-placed Rangers. The table read, Hibernian: 48 points, 78 goals for, 26 against; Rangers: 38 points, 64 goals for, 37 against. The triumph contained a sequence of nine wins in a row, followed later by a 16-game run involving just one defeat (against Airdrie). Hibs' last two league fixtures saw them paired against the 'Old Firm' and winning both matches (4-1 versus Rangers on April 28; 3-1 versus Celtic, two days later).

The season before (1949/50), Hibs had finished second, but not before running

Picture Gallery

Barry Lavety

Darren Jackson

Gordon Hunter celebrates scoring the goal that broke Hearts' 22-game unbeaten run in the Edinburgh Derby. August 27th, 1994.

Keith Wright

Ray Wilkins

Kevin Harper

Michael Weir

Murdo MacLeod

Skol Cup Winning Team, 1991.

High-flyer Graham Mitchell in the Skol Cup Final v Dunfermline, 1991.

League Cup Winners 1972

League Cup and Drybrough Cup winning squad, 1972.

Alex Miller

Jocky Scott

Jim Duffy

Alex McLeish

Pat Stanton, Eddie Turnbull & Alan Gordon with the Drybrough Cup.

Bobby Johnstone

Lawrie Reilly

Smith, Johnstone, Reilly & Turnbull . . . Four of the Famous Five in more recent times, with former Hibs Chairman, David Duff, and former Chief Executive, Jim Gray.

Hibs v Vascu Du Gama.

Willie Ormond

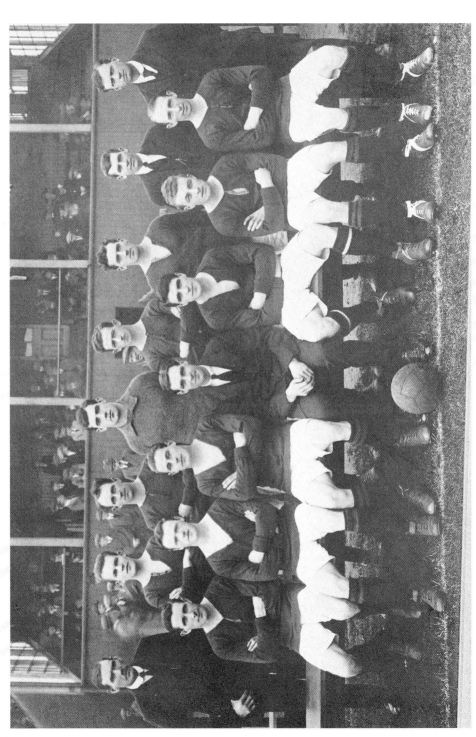

The Early Days

Some familiar faces in this sixties squad.

Hibs squad in the 20's.

First Division Champions, 1981/82.

Joe Baker returns to Easter Road at the Hands off Hibs Rally

Another goal for Hibs.

Pat McGinlay.

The realisation of relegation hits Willie Miller.

Rangers close. After losing 5-2 at Tynecastle in the second game of the campaign, Hibs proceeded to pick up 25 out of a possible 26 points. However, another 'derby' defeat - on January 2, in front of the biggest-ever crowd at Easter Road (65,850) - plus silly dropped points elsewhere, allowed Rangers to re-enter the frame during the closing stages.

Hibs' last game was, ironically, against Rangers at Ibrox, on April 29. It ended 0-0. It was not enough. Rangers, with a game in hand, secured the point they needed to take the title, thanks to a hard-fought match against Third Lanark, which finished 2-2 but could have ended in defeat had 'Thirds' converted a late penalty.

Hibs' third title win (season 1951/52) immediately followed the second. Though not as sparkling as the season before, it was still fairly solid, with Hibs finishing four points clear. They did, however, score a barrowload of goals. This time, the table read, Hibernian: 45 points, 92 goals for and 36 goals against; runners-up Rangers: 41 points, 61 goals for and 31 goals against.

Mind you, for goals, the next season was even better. But for all their 93 goals, it was not enough to prevent Hibs being pipped at the post by Rangers, losing a third-successive title on 'goal average' (Rangers' average was 2.051; Hibs' was 1.823. In those days, a 3-1 win was - in 'average' terms - better than an a 8-3 win)

The glaring omission from such notable achievements is success in the Scottish Cup. Hibs appeared in two Scottish Cup Finals between 1947 (there was no Cup Final in 1946) and the retirement of the last of the *Five*, Ormond, in 1961. On neither occasion, did the *Famous Five* line up in entirety. Smith, Turnbull and Ormond played in the 2-1 defeat by Aberdeen in April, 1947. In 1958, only Turnbull and Ormond played. During the intervening years, Hibs' great knack was to lose semi finals at Tynecastle. Or, lose so early on in the competition that a series of glamour 'friendlies' against English opposition had to be played to while away the time.

In the League Cup, it was little better. Turnbull was the only absentee when Hibs lined up against Motherwell in the final of October 28, 1950. Yet, despite having inflicted a 6-2 league defeat on the Fir Park club (on their own patch, too) a fortnight earlier, they still managed to lose 3-0. It didn't help that both Smith and Reilly were unfit.

Hibs lost at the semi-final stage of the League Cup during seasons 1946/47, 1949/50, 1952/53 and 1953/54. Again, Tynecastle represented something of a hoodoo venue.

Less glaring, but every bit as poignant, was Hibs' close-run thing in the European Cup. When Hibs travelled to Brazil for a summer tour in 1953 - making such a favourable impression that the team was held up as a model for the Brazilian national team to learn from - they were widely regarded as the most European club in Britain. In chairperson, Harry Swan, they had one of the most progressive thinkers in the game. Therefore, when it came to handing out invitations to take part in the inaugural European Cup, there was no hesitation that Hibs should be among those hand-picked elite. It meant that Eddie Turnbull became the first Briton to score in European competition (by the way, another of Turnbull's claims to fame is that he is one of the few players ever to have scored a 'hat-trick' of penalties in one game, against Celtic in February, 1950 – he actually scored four, the other goal coming from open play).

The problem, however, was that Hibs were already beginning to pass their prime. Being season 1955/56, Johnstone was already gone and though the club reached the semi finals, losing to a Rheims side inspired by its own legendary figure, Raymond Kopa, the consensus is that had the tournament been introduced five years earlier, Hibs would have been sure-fire winners. Such an achievement would not have flattered the *Famous Five*.

Gordon Smith fact-file. Born: Edinburgh, May 25, 1924. Height: 5'9". Weight: 11st 10lbs. Honours: 18 Scotland caps, one Scottish war-time international cap, numerous Scottish schoolboy caps, 10 Scottish League caps, five Scottish League Championship medals, one Scottish Cup runners-up medal, one League Cup runners-up medal.

Lawrie Reilly fact-file. Born: Edinburgh, October 28, 1928. Height: 5'7". Weight: 10st 6lbs. Honours: 38 Scotland caps, 13 Scottish League caps, two League Championship medals, one League Cup runners-up medal.

Bobby Johnstone fact-file. Born: Selkirk, September 7, 1929. Height: 5'7". Weight: 10st 7lbs. Honours: 13 Scotland caps, six Scottish League caps, one Great Britain v Rest of Europe appearance, three Scottish League Championship medals, one Scottish Cup runners-up medal, one FA Cup winners medal, one FA Cup runners-up medal.

Eddie Turnbull fact-file. Born: Falkirk, April 12, 1923. Height: 5'8". Weight: 11st. Honours: eight Scotland caps, one Scotland 'B' cap, four Scottish League caps, three Scottish League Championship medals, two Scottish Cup runners-up medals.

Willie Ormond fact-file. Born: Falkirk, February 23, 1927; died May 4, 1984. Height: 5'7". Weight: 10st 10lbs. Honours: six Scotland caps, one Scotland 'B' cap, 10 Scottish League caps, three Scottish League Championship medals, two Scottish Cup runners-up medals, one League Cup runners-up medal. Awarded the OBE after guiding Scotland to an unbeaten campaign during the finals of the 1974 World Cup.

CUP OF WOE?
HIBS IN THE
SCOTTISH CUP

IF THERE is anything that makes a Hibs fan squirm with embarrassment, it is the club's lack of silverware in the Scottish Cup. In not having won the competition since 1902, they are at risk of setting a bizarre record of under-achievement.

Since 1902, when Hibs defeated Celtic 1-0, the 'Old Firm' have shared the Scottish Cup 52 times. But a further 15 clubs have stepped in when the 'Old Firm' have stepped out.

All the more galling is the fact that Hibs have been mighty close to repeating that auspicious victory of 1902 when, on April 26, Andy McGeachan's goal secured the trophy and laid the foundations for a comfortable title win the following season. But whether favourites or underdogs, it has always been a case of so near, yet so far.

Hibs' first Cup win occurred even earlier: in 1887, courtesy of a 2-1 win over Dumbarton, doubly significant because it was the first time the trophy had left the West of Scotland since the competition began in season 1873/74.

Newspaper reports from the time differ as to the Hibs scorers, but there is no doubt as to the source of the winner, Willie Groves dribbling his way into the heart of the Dumbarton defence before hitting the ball home.

Though Groves' playing career at Hibs was relatively short and, despite being among a group of Hibs players who signed up controversially to the newly-created Celtic (formed in 1888), he was, nevertheless, a darling figure.

In total, Hibs have won the competition twice and finished runner-up eight times, the last time in 1979, when it took three games before Rangers - with the help of an Arthur Duncan own-goal - vanquished Hibs, after the first two games had ended goalless.

In 1914, it required a replay before Celtic won 4-1. In 1923 and 1924, exactly the same Hibs team contested the finals against Celtic and Airdrio, losing 1-0 and 2-0 respectively.

In the first post-war final, despite going a goal up in the first minute, Hibs were eventually to lose against Aberdeen. Eleven years later, Hibs played the 1958 Cup Final as favourites against Clyde, only to lose 1-0.

Then in 1972, in front of a staggering 106,000 fans, a side that had just come under the managerial wing of Eddie Turnbull and who were later to become one of the best-ever Hibs sides, capitulated to Celtic, losing 6-1. It wasn't the heaviest defeat incurred by Hibs in the competition (a 9-1 defeat by Dumbarton on September 27, 1890 accounts for that particular record) but it certainly was one of the most painful.

Between the Cup victories in 1887 and 1902, there was a final against Hearts, played at Logie Green, near Powderhall, in Edinburgh. It finished Hearts 3 Hibernian 1.

In 1923, Hibs went all the way to the final without conceding a goal.

Not often, but sometimes, Hibs have done all the hard work before slipping up in comparatively easy situations. It is a tale of woe to have similarly bedevilled some of Hibs' efforts in Scotland's other major cup competition, the League Cup (though wins in 1972 and 1991 go some way towards soothing the hurt in that knock-out event).

Of the many classic games between Hibs and the 'Old Firm', one of the most thrilling was against Rangers on February 10, 1951, which saw Hibs and their *Famous Five* forward line at their very best, beating the 'Light Blues' on their own turf, 3-2. This was a clash of the undisputed top two clubs in the country and it was goals from Gordon Smith, Eddie Turnbull and Bobby Johnstone which sealed the win in front of a 100,000-plus crowd.

It was a game when Hibs had to twice come back from behind. Johnstone's winner just happened to be a stylish overhead kick.

But then what do Hibs go on to do? After defeating Airdrie in the quarter final, they lose to Motherwell in the 'semis', going down 3-2 at Tynecastle, which, for a while, proved something of a hoodoo venue as far as cup semi finals were concerned. Other semi-final setbacks at the stadium include Rangers in season 1928/29, Clyde in 1938/39, Dunfermline in 1964/65 and Aberdeen in 1992/93.

Sometimes, there are no excuses but nevertheless, some valiant efforts, not least Hibs versus Aberdeen on February 2, 1957. It was the fifth round of the competition and, by half-time, Hibs were an amazing 4-0 down.

Even though the game proved finally beyond them, the scale of the fightback was impressive. Shooting down the Easter Road slope, Hibs clawed their way back to 4-3, with goals from Gordon Smith, Lawrie Reilly and Bobby Nicol. However, the grandstand finish teed up by the scoring spree came to nothing, with the final agony being an effort by Willie Ormond, that would have levelled the scores, hitting the crossbar.

However, there have been some defeats that are beyond soothing words. On January 22, 1938, amateur side, Edinburgh City, inflicted a real piece of giant-killing when they defeated Hibs 3-2. Says Brian Mark, a Hibernian historian: "*It was a real disaster for Hibs, on a par with Rangers' defeat in 1967 by Berwick Rangers. City took their chances while Hibs squandered theirs, even missing a penalty kick.*" The long odds offered by the bookies made some people a nice little earner.

And what about the scoreline of March 2, 1977? Hibernian 1 Arbroath 2, in a fourth round replay. Or the game against Ayr United, played on Sunday, February 17, 1980 at

Easter Road. Though Hibs won, 2-0, the big story was the news that the legendary but mischievous George Best - signed the previous November - was sacked (in the wake of a drinking spree), a decision which, thankfully, was rescinded.

Or, the 5-0 defeat by Hearts on February 5, 1955, which included all five of the *Famous Five* (Gordon Smith, Bobby Johnstone, Lawrie Reilly, Eddie Turnbull and Willie Ormond) and the 'sixth' member, Bobby Combe. The only notable absentee was goalkeeper, Tommy Younger.

The Matchday Programme's summary of the game read: "*In their moment of glory, Hearts players and supporters joined the critics in congratulating Gordon Smith on a magnificent match. Although on the losing side, Gordon pulled out almost every trick in the book, but unfortunately for Hibs, there was no-one who could turn his superb leading up into goals*". The run-up to Hibs' Cup Final appearance in 1958 centres on Hibs' goalscoring sensation, Joe Baker, the last great signing by manager Hugh Shaw. Having required a replay to sweep Dundee United aside in the second round, Hibs' next opponents were none other than rivals, Hearts, riding on a high, having finished second to Rangers in the league the previous season.

At Tynecastle, Hearts scored three times. But Hibs scored four times, with each goal netted by a 17-year old Baker.

Interviewed in the Hibernian Matchday Programme of December 15, 1995, Baker - who won three Scotland schoolboy caps, six England under-23 caps and eight full England caps - said: "*We were definitely the underdogs that day, Hearts were a very strong team, with players such as Dave Mackay in their side.*

"*The funny thing, though, at the time was that I never realised the full significance of it all. It was just my job.*

"*So when I scored four against Hearts, I never really thought too much about it. You would have to go to the newspaper cuttings to see how the goals were scored, I can't remember the details. I was only 17 at the time and because I lived in the west, I was off home after a shower.*

"*Against Hearts, we didn't go out with any particular tactic. Hughie Shaw just said, 'Go out and play', and that's what we did. We gave them a real roasting that day. What I did really only dawned on me the following Monday.*"

Hibs reached the final, against Clyde. But having previously been the hero, Baker then turned villain. He admits himself: he was too nervous.

Two years later, Baker was truly among the goals. On February 11, Hibernian were drawn against Peebles Rovers in the second round. By full-time, the score was 15-1 (a club record) and Joe Baker had scored nine of the goals (another club record).

Of a more recent vintage is the quarter-final tie at Easter Road on March 8, 1986 between Hibs and Celtic. It is not just the last-gasp 4-3 victory that stands out, but the fact that it was the second cup victory recorded by Hibs over Celtic that season. Seven months previously, in the League Cup, Hibs and Celtic could not be separated after extra time, the score standing at a breathtaking 4-4. In the 'penalty shoot-out', Hibs managed to do enough, winning 4-3.

Since their last appearance in the final, Hibs have reached five semi finals, losing each of them. In season 1979/80 (the season they were relegated to the First Division), they lost 5-0 to Celtic. Then there was the semi-final loss to Aberdeen at Dens Park on April 5, 1986. Three years later, it was a 3-1 loss, again to Celtic at Hampden Park (when new owner, David Duff, did a rather ostentatious walkabout among the fans). At Tynecastle, on April 3, 1993, Aberdeen were the 1-0 victors. Two years later, it took a replay (after the first game finished 0-0) before Celtic defeated Hibs 3-1.

Remarkably, the semi-final win that took Hibs to the 1978/79 final was watched by just under 10,000 people. In the first game of the final, had an attempted save by Rangers' goalkeeper, Peter McCloy, at the feet of Hibs' Colin Campbell been adjudged a penalty, there might not have been any need to play the other two matches.

The first replay ended in a fairly dull 0-0 draw, the same scoreline as the first head-to-head. The second ended 3-2 for Rangers, with a flying header by Arthur Duncan (that went in to his own net) handing Rangers the crucial, third goal (in extra time).

Inevitably, just as there have been some great Cup matches between Hibs and Celtic, so too with the other half of the 'Old Firm'. Fifteen years earlier, Jock Stein - who was Hibs manager all too briefly before leaving Easter Road to manage Celtic - steered Hibs to a remarkable trio of wins over the Ibrox side in season 1964/65, the last of them being in the Cup when the mercurial Willie Hamilton was again king.

By the time it came to the third round of the Cup on March 6, Edinburgh was buzzing with anticipation. A crowd of 47,000 squeezed into Easter Road to witness a narrow 2-1 win, just as the game seemed destined for a 1-1 draw and a replay in Glasgow. But with 89 minutes on the clock, Hibs' John Fraser floated in a free-kick for Hamilton to steer home (albeit with the faintest of touches that may, in truth, have been no touch all, despite Hamilton's claim that it was his goal).

There was similarly a buzz of excitement when Hibs met Aberdeen in the first post-war final in 1947 - April 19. Hibs' passage included the longest Cup semi final ever played, lasting a remarkable 142 minutes before a lobbed goal from Hugh Howie settled things against Motherwell. The reason for the game being strung out so long? Post-war austerity meant games had to be played to a finish.

One of the deepest sadnesses surrounding Hibs' participation in the Scottish Cup was the collapse and death of Willie McCartney, in the wake of a comfortable win against Albion Rovers in January 1948. A charismatic manager, it was McCartney who spotted the talent to create the *Famous Five*. It was McCartney who laid the foundations for Hibs' three League Championship wins in the late 1940s and early 1950s.

In a 'souvenir pictorial' of Hibernian published at the end of season 1948/49, McCartney is described as *"first and foremost, a man of vision"*.

There would be no better tribute to him than Hibs finally winning the trophy that proved so tantalisingly beyond even McCartney's carefully-crafted teams.

Hibs in the Scottish Cup

February 12, 1887: Hibernian 2 (Montgomery, Groves) Dumbarton 1 Team: J Tobin, J Lundie, Fagan, P McGinn, J McGhee, J McLaren, P Lafferty, Montgomery, Groves, Clark, Smith. Played at Hampden Park.

March 14, 1896: Hearts 3 Hibernian 1 (O'Neill) Team: McColl, Robertson, McFarlane, Breslin, Neill, Murphy, P Murphy, Kennedy, Groves, W Smith, O'Neill. Played at Logie Green.

April 26, 1902: Hibernian 1 (McGeachan) Celtic 0 Team: Rennie, Gray, Breslin, Harrower, Robertson, McCall, McGeachan. Divers, Callaghan, Atherton. Played at Celtic Park.

April 11, 1914: Celtic 0 Hibernian 0 Team: Allan, Girdwood, Templeton, Kerr, Paterson, Grosert, Wilson, Fleming, Hendren, Woods, Smith. Played at Ibrox.

April 16, 1914: Replay Celtic 4 Hibernian 1 (Smith) Team: Allan, Girdwood, Templeton, Kerr, Paterson, Grosert, Wilson, Fleming, Hendren, Woods, Smith. Played at Ibrox.

March 31, 1923: Celtic 1 Hibernian 0 Team: W Harper, W McGinnigle, W Dornan, P Kerr, W Miller, H Shaw, H Ritchie, J Dunn, J McColl, J Halligan, J Walker. Played at Hampden Park.

April 19, 1924: Airdrie 2 Hibernian 0 Team: W Harper, W McGinnigle, W Dornan, P Kerr, W Miller, H Shaw, H Ritchie, J Dunn, J McColl, J Halligan, J Walker. Played at Ibrox.

April 19, 1947: Aberdeen 2 Hibernian 1 (Cuthbertson) Team: J Kerr, J Govan, D Shaw, H Howie, P Aird, S Kean, G Smith, WG Finnigan, JG Cuthbertson, E Turnbull, W Ormond. Played at Hampden Park.

April 26, 1958: Clyde 1 Hibernian 0 Team: L Leslie, J Grant, J McClelland, E Turnbull, J Plenderleith, J Baxter, J Fraser, A Aitken, J Baker, T Preston, W Ormond. Played at Hampden Park.

May 6, 1972: Celtic 6 Hibernian 1 (Gordon) Team: J Herriot, J Brownlie, E Schaedler, P Stanton, J Black, J Blackley, A Edwards, J Hazel, A Gordon, J O'Rourke, A Duncan, (R Auld). Played at Hampden Park.

May 12, 1979: Rangers 0 Hibernian 0 Team: J McArthur, A Brazil, A Duncan, D Bremner, G Stewart, J McNamara, R Hutchinson, (G Rae), A MacLeod, C Campbell, R Callachan, A Higgins. Played at Hampden Park.

May 16, 1979: First Replay Rangers 0 Hibernian 0 (after extra time) Team: J McArthur, A Brazil, A Duncan, D Bremner, G Stewart, J McNamara, G Rae, A MacLeod, C Campbell, R Callachan, A Higgins, (S Brown). Played at Hampden Park.

May 28, 1979: Second Replay Rangers 3 Hibernian 2 (after extra time) (Higgins, MacLeod, pen). Team: J McArthur, A Brazil, A Duncan, D Bremner, G Stewart, J McNamara, G Rae, A MacLeod, C Campbell, R Callachan, (S Brown), A Higgins (R Hutchinson). Played at Hampden Park.

TURNBULL'S TORNADOES

WHEN IT comes to natural choices, there was no-one better equipped to take over the job as Hibs manager at the start of the 1970s than Eddie Turnbull. As one of the *Famous Five* forward line of the late 1940s and early 1950s, his name was inextricably linked with, undoubtedly, the most successful era in the club's entire history.

As part of the *Five* - consisting of Gordon Smith, Bobby Johnstone, Lawrie Reilly, Eddie Turnbull and Willie Ormond - he was part of the Easter Road fabric when the club finished League Champions three times within the space of just five years.

As a manager, he had already earned his spurs. He had left Hibs in the early 1960s to move into coaching with Queen's Park. From there, he took up the reigns at Aberdeen, during which time he won a Scottish Cup, making the 'Dons' a force to be reckoned with.

At both Pittodrie and Easter Road, he was a man to excite fierce loyalty and loathing. Some players hated his sharp tongue, others were awe-struck by his wisdom and deep understanding of the game.

Explaining his part in a goal against Wales that helped Scotland through to the 1978 World Cup in Argentina, Martin Buchan, who left Aberdeen to become captain of Manchester United, said: *"I was a substitute, I came on for only 12 minutes to replace Sandy Jardine, and although I'd never played the position before, I knew exactly what to do because of the teaching of Eddie Turnbull when he was my manager at Aberdeen.*

"I knew where I should have been at any given time. And there was a move in midfield and I was there in the space to take the ball on the right wing. I was in the space because my brain told me I should be there, not because I was a raiding fullback." (Buchan's cross was headed by Dalglish to make it 2-0, to seal Scotland's qualification).

Twice since Hibs' founding in 1875, there have been two eras so rich in colour and achievement that all it takes is the shorthand of a nickname to provoke instant and happy recognition. It was the *Famous Five* during the late 1940s and early 1950s. In the 1970s, the limelight belonged to *Turnbull's Tornadoes*.

If there is an argument that the era of the *Famous Five* was not properly rewarded with silverware, that is surely the case with the next generation of Hibs players deserving of their very own name-tag.

The previous decade - the 1960s - was one of mixed fortunes for Hibs, including some tremendous European nights but also a brush with relegation in season 1962/63, which had begun badly, with the first five league games yielding just one point (a 2-2 draw against Motherwell on September 15, 1962). There then followed a brief recovery before, again, the points proved frustratingly elusive.

The winter of 1962/63 was one of the severest on record. Consequently, as late as

March 9, 1963, Hibs had still 17 league fixtures to complete. Before they knew it, however, they found themselves trailing third-bottom Clyde by eight points, albeit with three games in hand over the Shawfield club.

As the run-in began to hot up, Hibs then faced four home games in ten days. Two wins and a draw meant that Hibs stood on 18 points from 29 games, Clyde on 22 points from 30 games.

And so to the Edinburgh derby of May 3. With Clyde's last two fixtures against the 'Old Firm', Hibs had to get something from the game to give themselves any chance of survival. At 2-0 down at half-time, it looked all over. But three second-half goals in five minutes earned a 3-3 draw.

While Clyde were themselves stuttering, Hibs moved within two points (with a game in hand but inferior 'goal average') thanks to a 2-1 win over St Mirren on May 11. A 4-0 win over Queen of the South soon after meant they were level on points and, as crucially, sitting on a superior 'goal average'.

Hibs' last game was before Clyde's (whose penultimate match had ended with a 2-0 defeat by Celtic). It was against Raith Rovers, already relegated and managed by former Hibs boss, Hugh Shaw. It ended 4-0 to Hibs. To leapfrog Hibs in the table, Clyde had to defeat Rangers by nine goals. They lost, 3-1. Hibs were safe and, throughout the campaign, owed much to the goalkeeping excellence of Ronnie Simpson. Another hero was Gerry Baker - brother of Joe - whose 'hat-trick' against Dundee on April 8 was a vital piece in the jigsaw of recovery.

But the trauma exacted a price. After 30 years as chairman, Harry Swan, sold the club on - to Bill Harrower. And in the spring of 1964, Walter Galbraith resigned, to be succeeded a short while later by Jock Stein. The Summer Cup of 1964 hinted at what Stein would later achieve as manager of Celtic.

Towards the end of the decade - by which time Stein had long gone to be succeeded, first by Bob Shankly (brother of Liverpool's Bill), then Willie McFarlane - Hibs had the honour of playing a League Cup Final. But on October 28, 1969, goals from Jimmy O'Rourke and Eric Stevenson in front of a 74,000 crowd at Hampden were not enough to prevent Celtic winning 6-2.

Hibs' best league placing that decade was at the end of season 1967/68 when they finished third to Celtic and Rangers. Mind you, the gap between Hibs and runners-up, Rangers, was a massive 16 points.

Turnbull joined Hibs as manager on July 12, 1971, ten months after Tom Hart - otherwise known as 'Mr Hibs' because of his passion for the club - had taken control at Easter Road.

His six years at Aberdeen meant he had been previously linked with the Hibs job whenever it fell vacant. In the end, he succeeded Dave Ewing, manager for less than a year after the extrovert McFarlane had been sacked on the night of December 9, 1970, when Hibs were due to play Liverpool in the first leg, third round of the Fairs Cup.

One of Turnbull's first tasks was to recruit a new goalkeeper, sending out the feelers as far as South Africa, where former Dunfermline goalkeeper, Jim Herriot, was based.

With Jim soon on board, it was back to Dunfermline again, but this time more directly, for the next major signing. For just £12,000, Alex Edwards, a midfield maestro, proved one of the bargains of the decade. His arrival was quickly followed by that of Alan Gordon, from Dundee United.

Little by little, the team began to come together. Most, of course, were players recruited during previous regimes, not least that of Walter Galbraith, the manager who signed Pat Stanton, the captain during the club's centenary year in 1975 and later to become Hibs manager himself.

However, the mould was not quite set when the club found itself facing the test of a vibrant Celtic side in the Scottish Cup Final on May 6, 1972, in front of a crowd of 106,000 at Hampden.

On the way, Hibs had dispatched Partick Thistle (2-0), Airdrie (2-0), Aberdeen (2-0, in the quarter final) and Rangers (2-0 in a replayed semi final after the first game ended 1-1). In other words, Hibs had conceded just the one goal.

Celtic's route included a 5-0 win over Albion Rovers and a 4-0 win over Dundee and they were in the goals again against Hibs. Alan Gordon got one for Hibs, but, for Celtic, Dixie Deans got three, Lou Macari grabbed two and Billy McNeill nicked one.

6-1. It was a result that needed overturning as soon as possible, to prevent the wound becoming a mortal blow. In three months, it was mission accomplished as Hibs defeated Celtic in the traditional pre-season tournament, the Drybourgh Cup, even though they allowed a 3-0 lead to slip from their grasp, having to play extra time at 3-3 before winning 5-3 through goals from Jimmy O'Rourke and Arthur Duncan.

A few months later, it was time for the League Cup to wing its way to Edinburgh.

The build-up to this latest cup triumph had seen Hibs finish second to Aberdeen in their qualifying section, having played six, won five and lost once (to Aberdeen at Pittodrie). After that, there was no looking back. An aggregate 5-2 win over Dundee United (over two legs) was followed by an even more emphatic aggregate win in the quarter finals, 10-3 over Airdrie (again, over two legs). Only Rangers stood in the way of a place in the final and, thanks to a solo goal from right-back John Brownlie (who raced almost an entire half of the field before netting), the 'Light Blues' were, likewise, swept aside.

Pat Stanton scores in the League Cup Final against Celtic.

The scoreline on December 9, 1972 reads Hibernian 2 Celtic 1. The pre-match tactical jousting between Turnbull and his opposite number, Jock Stein, led to Celtic playing Jimmy Johnstone in the unusual position of outside left to curb Brownlie's attacking prowess (normally, 'Jinky' was posted on the right to torment defenders!).

The win was less narrow than the one-goal margin suggests. Hibs were 2-0 up, thanks to goals from Pat Stanton and Jimmy O'Rourke, and cruising before Celtic started to make any headway. It was by way of consolation that Kenny Dalglish scored for Celtic, who, at this time in their history, were beginning to make a habit of losing League Cup Finals (after defeating Hibs and St Johnstone in the 1968/69 and 1969/70 finals, Celtic proceeded to lose the next four, to Rangers 1-0, Partick Thistle 4-1, Hibs 2-1 and Dundee 1-0).

The League Cup victory was proof positive that Hibs were more than one-hit wonders. On the day the silverware was paraded at Easter Road - December 16 - Ayr United were the hapless victims of an 8-1 celebration scoreline.

Just as the *Famous Five* of Smith, Johnstone, Reilly, Turnbull and Ormond has a poetic ring to it, so, too, the League Cup Final line-up of Jim Herriot, John Brownlie, Erich Schaedler, Pat Stanton, Jim Black, John Blackley, Alex Edwards, Jimmy O'Rourke, Alan Gordon, Alex Cropley and Arthur Duncan.

It is no surprise, therefore, that the team that was to play Hearts less than a month later in the Ne'erday 'derby' was exactly the same. The venue was Tynecastle. The Hibernian scorers were Gordon x2, O'Rourke x2, Duncan x2 and Cropley. Score 7-0 (half-time 5-0).

All the more remarkable, Hibs had needed six goals to go to the top of Division One. They did so with a goal to spare.

The first goal came from O'Rourke, latching on to a Schaedler throw-in to crack a close-range shot. The second came from Gordon, taking an Edwards' pass on to his chest at the edge of the penalty area before slotting coolly home. Number three arrived courtesy of Duncan, capitalising on an intelligent interception by Cropley to steer the

1972/73 Hibernian Squad.

ball under Hearts' goalkeeper, Kenny Garland. It was Cropley himself who made it four, with a 20-yard volley. Duncan headed a fifth, O'Rourke tapped a Stanton shot to make it six and 'seventh heaven' was found when Gordon headed a Duncan cross.

Reporting the match, journalist Hugh Taylor in *The Daily Record*, began: "*Hibs sprinkled the stardust of super soccer all over Tynecastle. And with magic touches reminiscent of Real Madrid, Brazil and the unforgettable Hungarians, they climbed to the top of the First Division.*"

He added: "*This was football with speed, artistry and arrogance. This was glamorous, glittering football that had a huge crowd of 36,000 fans entranced.*"

Stewart Brown, in *The Edinburgh Evening News*, remarked: "*Unstoppable Hibs are the team of the moment - and the team of the future; so full of football, loaded with confidence and talent."* He noted that had Garland not brought off three excellent stops to deny Stanton, Gordon and O'Rourke, it might have been a *"double-figure tale of woe"* for Hearts. The win meant Hibs had gone 14 games against Hearts without defeat.

Rikki Raginia, one of Hibs' most respected historians, adds: *"For those not lucky enough to see the 'Famous Five' play, 'Turnbull's Tornadoes' were the best-ever Hibs side. They just could not stop scoring goals. As they were smashing eight past Ayr in December, they were already passing the 100 mark as far as goals - in all competitions - was concerned. For goals, what more could anyone ask?"*

Sadly, though, the game following the 'derby day' delight against Hearts proved, in retrospect, a turning point to the season. It was against East Fife - managed by ex-'Hibee', Pat Quinn - and two calamities befell the club.

First, John Brownlie's leg was broken in a clash with opposition player, Ian Printy. Second, in a fit of frustration, Alex Edwards threw the ball at an East Fife player to earn a caution that, once added to previous misdemeanours, earned a whopping 56-day suspension (taking in eight games).

The 1-0 win (scorer, Alan Gordon) on the day proved something of a Pyrrhic victory given the loss of Brownlie and Edwards during the following games. Had that wonderful Hibs team been able to stay intact, they might well have held on to the division's top spot all the way to the end of the season.

But the final league table for 1972/73 season showed Hibs finishing third, behind winners, Celtic, and runners-up, Rangers. It read: Celtic P34 W26 D5 L3 F93 A28 Pts57; Rangers P34 W26 D4 L4 F74 A30 Pts56; Hibernian P34 W19 D7 L8 F74 A33 Pts45.

Instead of a league title to celebrate that summer, there was another Drybrough Cup triumph, won just before the start of the next campaign. Unlike twelve months previously, however, the final was a tight affair, Alan Gordon scoring in the last minute of extra time to give Hibs a 1-0 win over Celtic.

By now, Hibernian FC were one of the classiest acts in not just Scotland but the whole of Britain, and season 1973/74 saw them in the title fight almost 'til the end. Doing one better than the year before, they finished runners-up, to Celtic. The final table read: Celtic P34 W23 D7 L4 F82 A27 Pts53; Hibernian P34 W20 D9 L5 F75 A42 Pts 49.

The following season, they would again finish runners-up, this time to Rangers, and again on 49 points.

Between seasons 1971/72 and 1974/7, Hibs finished fourth, third, second and second. And in the first season of the Premier Division, 1975/76, they finished third.

Such consistency might have been better served had the squads not been prone to fairly considerable change over the years.

Players celebrate with the Drybrough Cup.

Six months after the second Drybrough Cup win, Turnbull moved swiftly to sign former Aberdeen forward, Joe Harper, then playing for Everton. Money seemed to be no object in the manager's determination to net the striker. Nor a concern voiced in other quarters that the player was overweight.

The result was a £120,000 move from Merseyside, not only a club record at the time, but a Scottish record. The fee had been partly inflated by Aberdeen's interest in bringing the player back to the north east.

Harper's arrival had the knock-on effect of pushing other players - including the popular Jimmy O'Rourke - out of the door, either to generate money or make way for him. Not even a 'hat-trick' in the League Cup Final of 1974 - October 26 - could exonerate Joe in the eyes of some Hibs fans. And anyway, Hibs still lost, 6-3.

Though Alex Cropley was transferred to Arsenal, many of the other changes to the team that won the '72 League Cup were beyond Turnbull's control: Brownlie was injured, Alex Edwards was sitting in the stand (because of suspensions) more often than he was playing, Jim Black was nearing the end of his career and Jim Herriot had disobeyed managerial orders when Hibs played Yugoslav side, Hajduk Split, in the quarter final of the 1972/73 Cup Winners' Cup.

Even the stalwart Pat Stanton would be gone long before Turnbull finally took his leave of Easter Road, in the wake of a 5-0 defeat by Celtic in the semi final of the Scottish Cup, on April 12, 1980.

Pat Stanton scores to give Hibs a 1-0 lead in the 1972 Scottish Cup Semi Final v Rangers.

In 1976, Stanton teamed up with Stein at Celtic, collecting a richly-deserved League Championship medal plus a Scottish Cup winners' medal.

In total, Pat won 16 Scotland caps, though it is widely agreed he deserved many more. He made his international debut against Holland in 1966 and went on to captain his country three times. He has also played more European ties for Hibs than anyone else.

Clearly, though, Turnbull believed the League Cup team of 1972 lacked that extra special ingredient to turn them from runners-up to winners. As one of the best-ever managers in Scotland, his special gift was to detect weaknesses in individual players and team formations.

Certainly, Hibs' failure to defend a 4-2 first-leg lead against Hajduk Split, exasperated Turnbull. Hibs, he felt, had let a golden opportunity slip by losing 3-0 in the return.

Stanton's departure was, sadly, preceded by the disappointment of becoming increasingly peripheral to the manager's plans, including being dropped for a Euro game against Liverpool - on September 30, 1975 - in the wake of an embarrassing League Cup defeat by lowly Montrose six days' previously.

After being dropped for the Liverpool game, Pat was forced to sit out a further four league games before being recalled for a fixture at Celtic, on October 18, 1975.

It seemed a tactical masterstroke by Turnbull as Hibs took a 2-0 lead. But with seven minutes remaining, the referee abandoned the game because of fog. Instead of the points being awarded to Hibs, the game was replayed - on December 10 - with Schaedler scoring in a 1-1 draw.

Pat's final game for the club was on August 28, 1976, when he came on as a replacement for George Stewart, in a 9-2 demolition of St Johnstone in the League Cup. In total, he had made 399 first-team appearances for Hibs and scored 50 goals, the very first of which was netted on his debut, all of 13 years previously, against Motherwell on October 5, 1963 (when he was aged 19, score: 4-3 to Motherwell).

Just like the *Famous Five* era, it is important to guard against the memory playing tricks. The Turnbull era lasted all the way until 1980, at which point another *Famous Five* legend, Willie Ormond, took over as manager, albeit briefly.

But, in truth, by the time the inaugural Premier Division was up and running, the *Tornadoes* were already beginning to break up. Though Hibs finished third at the conclusion of that season, they followed it up by going into steady decline.

That neighbours, Hearts, were in a worse position (being relegated at the end of the following season) could not disguise the fact that all was not well at Easter Road. From 1976/77 to 1979/80, Hibs finished sixth, fourth, fifth and tenth.

By finishing tenth, they were relegated for the first time since season 1930/31.

Not even the emergency measure of hiring the ageing-but-still-genius figure of George Best for a year could stop the slide.

Best was signed up by chairman Hart on a reported £2,000 per appearance - making a scoring debut in a 2-1 defeat by St Mirren on November 24, 1979 - and he even played a handful of games for Hibs after they were condemned to the First Division. His last game was against Falkirk on October 11, 1980, which Hibs won 2-0.

In Europe too, the years were less fruitful than they had previously been. In the seasons following the Hadjuk Split game, there were still thrilling encounters on the Euoropean stage - versus Leeds United (1973/74), Juventus (1974/75) and Liverpool (1975/76). But, equally, there were disappointing setbacks against Oesters Vaxjoe (1976/77) and Strasbourg (1978/79).

The late 1970s was perhaps a case of manager and chairman - both firm friends - staying at Hibs longer than they ought to have done. Turnbull was beginning to increasingly suffer from ill health and Hart's pockets were no longer as deep as they used to be. A series of bargain basement signings failed to re-ignite the glory days.

In season 1976/77, there was a dull 18 draws from 36 games. Little did Hibs know at the time, but things were going to get worse before they got better.

FIFTY POST-WAR PERSONALITIES WHO HAVE HELPED SHAPE HIBERNIAN

Joe Baker - Goalscorer supreme who had two spells with the club. Now a familiar face in the *Famous Five* stand at Easter Road. Won eight England caps, scored nine goals in one game (versus Peebles Rovers in the Scottish Cup) and holds the club record score of 42 goals in one season (season 1959/60). Played also for Torino, Arsenal, Nottingham Forest and Sunderland.

George Best - Signed by chairman Tom Hart in a bid to avoid relegation from the Premier Division in season 1979/80. Signed in November 1979, was away by the following October. On a reputed £2,000 per appearance. Though the club was still relegated, the ex-Manchester United and Northern Ireland genius brought colour and humour to an otherwise drab period in the club's history.

John Blackley - 'Sloop' has been a player, coach and manager at Easter Road. Was at the club as a player twice and throughout, he was a stalwart defender. Initially at the club during the late 1960s and 1970s. Then returned for a short stint during the early 1980s. His first spell ended when Hibs sold him to Newcastle United. Played in the 1974 World Cup finals for Scotland, during an international career that brought seven caps.

Des Bremner - Joined Hibs from Highland League side, Deveronvale, and made his mark as a right-back after John Brownlie was sidelined by a broken leg. However, he found his true position as hard-grafting midfield player. Like George Best, he won a European Cup medal (with Aston Villa). Won one Scotland cap, versus Switzerland in season 1975/76.

John Brownlie - Started off as a sweeper until he was played as a right-back at Muirton Park, Perth, in August 1971, when he came on as a substitute for Chris Shevlane and created two goals in a 3-1 win. From then on, he made the raiding right-back role his own. Rated among the best fullbacks in Britain. His rising career was desperately interrupted by a leg break sustained against East Fife one week after Hibs had demolished rivals, Hearts, 7-0 on January 1, 1973. Like John Blackley, Hibs sold him to Newcastle. Also like Blackley, he won seven Scotland caps. One low point was missing a penalty against Liverpool in the 1975/76 UEFA Cup. A high point was going on a solo run to score the only goal in the semi final of the 1971/1972 League Cup, between Hibs and Rangers.

John Collins - Won the first of his many Scotland caps while with Hibs (versus Saudi Arabia in season 1987/88) and though he has travelled far and wide since, always has a place in his heart for his first club. A tricky, left-sided midfielder, he was determined to continue his education at Easter Road longer than many pundits expected.

Bobby Combe - Had the *Famous Five* been known as the *Sensational Six*, Combe would have been the sixth man. A wing-half or inside forward, he gained three caps for Scotland and was one of Hibs' most versatile players during the 1950s. On retirement, he opened a grocer's shop in Edinburgh, near the foot of Leith Walk.

Peter Cormack - A cool customer always likely to spring a surprise. He left Easter Road in an £80,000 move to Nottingham Forest and was eventually to win honours with Liverpool. Like John Blackley, enjoyed two stints at Hibs, his second spell seeing him score his 100th league goal for the club. Famously, he scored against Real Madrid in a glamour 'friendly' organised by Hibs' manager at the time, Jock Stein. He was briefly assistant manager to Alex Miller at Easter Road and has managed elsewhere, including Partick Thistle and in Cyprus. Made his international debut (he won nine Scotland caps) against Brazil in June 1966.

Alex Cropley - 'Sojer' (because he was born in Aldershot), he was among the first players to qualify for Scottish international honours through parentage. Despite being prone to leg breaks, he was a classy left-sided midfielder during the 1970s and a key figure in *Turnbull's Tornadoes*. Transferred reluctantly to Arsenal, thereafter moving to Aston Villa. His two caps were scant recognition of his prodigious talents.

Joe Davis - Scored 51 goals as a left-back, 49 of them from the penalty spot. Signed from Third Lanark in the mid-60s as a replacement for John Parke (who moved to Sunderland). Skippered Hibs in a side that included Pat Stanton and Peter Cormack.

David Duff - Though David Duff's brief chairmanship of Hibs foundered on an attempted takeover of Hibs by his counterpart at rivals, Hearts, he did open the club to fans through a share issue. And he brought a touch of 'pizzazz' to Easter Road. A better-structured share issue, and Wallace Mercer's takeover attempt in 1990 might never have happened. However, in resisting the temptation to sell his own shareholding, he ensured Hibs' survival.

Arthur Duncan - A speed merchant on the wing and Hibs' longest-serving player, whose career at Easter Road spanned three decades (from the 1960s to the 1980s). Made 446 appearances (in all competitions) for the club. Signed from Partick Thistle. Made six Scotland appearances.

Alex Edwards - A bargain signing from Dunfermline, bought by manager Eddie Turnbull for £12,000. Provided the ammunition in *Turnbull's Tornadoes* team, though his disciplinary record marred what could have been a great international career.

Sir Tom Farmer - Just as Hibs required resurrecting in the 1890s and were thankful that, among others, a certain Philip Farmer was prepared to come to the club's rescue, so Hibs were grateful almost a century later when Sir Tom stepped in to help avert the club from going under, following an attempted takeover in 1990 by Wallace Mercer, then chairman of Hearts.

Alan Gordon - A tall, elegant, centre-forward, signed from South African side, Durban United. Became the spearhead of the *Turnbull's Tornadoes* team of the 1970s. Has the distinction of having played for both Edinburgh (Hibs and Hearts) and Dundee (Dundee and Dundee United) clubs. Is a qualified chartered accountant, practising in Edinburgh.

Jock Govan - An integral part of the League Championship-winning sides of the early 1950s. A right-back with flair in abundance. Won six Scotland caps.

Willie Hamilton - The typical Scottish footballing genius, where astounding talent is matched by a tendency to self-destruct. Signed from Hearts (for next to nothing) by Hibs manager Walter Galbraith. But it was under Galbraith's successor, Jock Stein, that Hamilton really flourished, during which time he won his one and only Scotland cap (versus Finland in Helsinki in a 1965 World Cup qualifying tie). Was transferred by Stein's successor, Bob Shankly, to Aston Villa, leaving a string of fond, quirky memories of his time at Easter Road.

Tom Hart - An East Lothian builder who sold his company to become 'Mr Hibs' during the 1970s. As chairman, taking over from Bill Harrower, he appointed Eddie Turnbull as manager and used his personal fortune to steer Hibs into the highest echelons of the game. Only Celtic, then managed by Jock Stein, stood in the way of Hibs being the top Scottish club.

Gordon Hunter - One of the many Hibs captains to be a fan. Gordon was a whole-hearted player who, among many achievements, scored the winner to break Hearts' 22-game unbeaten run in the Edinburgh 'derby'. Date: August 27, 1994.

Bobby Johnstone - One of the *Famous Five* and a magician with the ball. Sold to Manchester City in 1955, though he did return for nearly a year towards the end of his career (see *Famous Five* chapter).

Paul Kane - A whole-hearted 'Hibee' and, with dad Jimmy, among the many father and son combinations to have represented the club, others including Lew and Andy Goram, Allan and Mark McGraw, Joe McBride Snr and Jnr, and John and Craig Paterson.

Jimmy Kerr - A stalwart goalkeeper who was unlucky never to have won a cap. Became a Hibs director.

Bobby Kinloch - As historian Kenny Barclay remarks: *"The coolness he showed to score the winner from the penalty spot against Barcelona in the Fairs Cup [in season 1960/61] is enough on its own to put him in any Hibs Hall of Fame."*

Jim Leighton - With his career seemingly going nowhere, after being unceremoniously dropped by Manchester United, Hibs manager Alex Miller stepped in to provide a second chance, which Jim grabbed with both hands. The goalkeeper was an inspiration during the four years he was at the club, between 1993 and 1997. It meant a re-awakening of his Scotland career too.

Ally MacLeod - Signed from Southampton after starting his career at St Mirren (during which time he scored four goals against Rangers in a League Cup tie). He was a great goalscorer for Hibs in a side that was not up to very much. Had he been willing to co-operate more with George Best, he could have easily smashed the club's goals-in-one-season record of 42, held by Joe Baker. His skilful but languid style meant he was loved and hated by the fans in equal measure. For a while, set a Scottish record of scoring in eight consecutive league games (between March 11 and April 5, 1978). Capped three times at under-21 level (as an over-aged player).

Johnny MacLeod - Followed the same career path as Joe Baker during his first years in the game, joining Hibs from junior side, Armadale, before moving on to Arsenal. A skilful right-winger whose crosses led to a lot of Joe's many goals. Won four Scotland caps.

Murdo MacLeod - Hibs' inspirational captain when the club bounced back from an attempted takeover by Hearts chairman, Wallace Mercer, to win the Skol League Cup in 1991. Signed from Borussia Dortmund.

Willie McCartney - The dapper, charismatic Hibs manager who built the *Famous Five* side of the late 1940s and early 1950s but who was denied the pleasure of seeing the fruits of his labour, following a fatal collapse at the end of a Scottish Cup tie between Hibs and Albion Rovers in January 1948.

Jackie McNamara - When Jackie arrived at Easter Road from Celtic, it was to a chorus of disapproval, since the deal had involved the hugely popular Pat Stanton going the other way. However, he soon won over the support with his solid play and outstanding strength. After an outstanding performance against Newcastle United in a 'friendly', he played as sweeper.

John McNamee - 'Big' John, signed from Celtic by Hibs manager Jock Stein, was a powerful, commanding centre-half, always capable of getting on to the end of corners and free-kicks. A tremendous header of the ball, he was also headstrong at times, on one occasion sent-off in the 1965 League Cup semi-final, between Hibs and Celtic.

Neil Martin - Was about to give up football to become a lorry driver when manager, Walter Galbraith, stepped in to sign the Tranent-born inside-left for £7,000 from Queen of the South. Went from Hibs for £40,000 to Sunderland. Also played for Coventry and Nottingham Forest. Capped three times for Scotland. He was a powerful striker in the air and featured alongside Willie Hamilton in Scotland's 1965 World Cup qualifier in Finland.

Alex Miller - Appointed manager to replace John Blackley, Miller's career included dedicated service as a Rangers player and the manager's post at St Mirren. He proved similarly dedicated at Easter Road, his ten years at Hibs netting the 1991 Skol League Cup and two UEFA Cup campaigns.

Jimmy O'Rourke - Signed from Holy Cross Academy in Edinburgh and, just a kid, was an instant hit. A nippy player with a remarkable eye for goal. Made a scoring debut for Hibs versus Utrecht in 1962/63 Fairs Cup and proved particularly gifted at scoring goals in European competition. Was sold to St Johnstone in controversial circumstances, since he was having to make way for the recently-signed Joe Harper.

Willie Ormond - One of the *Famous Five* and, like Eddie Turnbull, to return to the club as manager (see *Famous Five* chapter).

Gordon Rae - Started off as a centre-forward, but quickly made the centre-half role his own. A 'Hibee' through and through, fully deserving of his testimonial year and match versus Manchester United. Became captain and, except for a short stint at Partick Thistle, was a truly one-club man. Signed from East of Scotland side, Whitehill Welfare, with whom he was a prolific goalscorer. Now manager of East of Scotland side, Edinburgh City.

Lawrie Reilly - 38 Scotland caps and 22 goals say it all about this goalscoring machine who spearheaded the *Famous Five* attack (see *Famous Five* chapter).

Alan Rough - Likeable goalkeeper who won 53 Scotland caps (though all bar two were when he was playing for Partick Thistle). Famously signed up by Hibs chairman, Kenny Waugh, while he (Waugh) was attending a boxing match. Kept goal with distinction during the 1980s and well-loved by the fans. As famous for his perms of the late 1970s.

Hugh Shaw - The most successful Hibs manager ever, even if the side that won three league titles under his leadership was as much the work of his predecessor, Willie McCartney. However, having to share the limelight ought not to diminish the stature of the man. Was previously a player and coach at Hibs. Retired to run a newsagent's in Edinburgh's Marchmont Road.

Ronnie Simpson - Goalkeeper par excellence, who made his senior debut in football in 1945 for Queen's Park at the tender age of 14 years and eight months. Was in the Celtic team that became the first from Britain to win the European Cup (in 1967, versus Inter Milan). At Hibs, his goalkeeping was a big factor in saving Hibs from relegation at the end of season 1962/63. At Newcastle United during the 1950s, he won two FA Cup winners' medals. His speciality was saving penalties. Signed for Hibs by manager, Hugh Shaw.

Gordon Smith - Arguably the most talented player ever to wear a Hibs jersey (see *Famous Five* chapter).

Pat Stanton - Being a relative of Michael Whelahan, the first Hibs captain, would have been fame enough for Pat, but his outstanding elegance on the field confirmed his place among the Hibs legends. Won 16 Scottish caps, though no-one doubts it ought to have been more. Joint top goalscorer in Europe for Hibs. Was played in midfield more than his more favoured defence and yet was still a star. Returned to manage the club and to display a great eye for a player.

Jock Stein - He wasn't Hibs manager for long, but his presence left an indelible impression. Thought big and, but for his sudden departure to Celtic in 1965, may well have guided the club to at least one trophy that season, even the league title. Did guide

Hibs to victory in the Summer Cup of 1964. Famously, he invited Real Madrid to play a 'friendly' at Easter Road, partly to test the calibre of his players, but mainly to test the ambition of the club's board of directors.

Eric Stevenson - Skilful left-winger, whose ability to dramatically fall in the penalty box helped establish Joe Davis' equally impressive penalty-scoring record. A firm favourite with the fans. Probably the best left-winger never to be capped.

George Stewart - Signed from Dundee. Another in the long line of Hibs-supporting captains. Was an assistant to Pat Stanton, when he was manager, along with Jimmy O'Rourke. Still an avid fan.

Harry Swan - One of the most innovative thinkers the game has ever had and, as Hibs chairman, the guiding light behind Hibs' status during the 1950s as one of the most progressive clubs in Britain. Under his stewardship, Hibs' ambitions knew few bounds. They would, for example, travel to the four corners of the globe during summer tours. He instigated Hibs' involvement in the first European Cup. His plans to expand Easter Road into a near-100,000 capacity stadium, didn't come off, but he did oversee the installation of floodlights.

Eddie Turnbull - A thunderbolt shot and, later, one of the club's most important managers (see *Famous Five* chapter).

Mickey Weir - From Hibs to Luton Town and back to Hibs, Mickey Weir could not be separated from the club of his boyhood dreams. A pocket dynamo with a heart of gold.

Keith Wright - Hibs-mad and, for a while, the most potent striker in the land, earning him a Scotland cap in season 1991/92 against Northern Ireland. After years of hoping he would play for his beloved club, he finally joined Hibs from Dundee in August 1991, becoming an instant hit, particularly for his part in bringing the Skol League Cup to Easter Road (where he scored in every round).

Tommy Younger - The goalkeeper who, because of national service in Germany during the early 1950s, made nearly 80 airline trips from the continent to play for Hibs. Was sold to Liverpool and also played for Leeds United. Made a personal fortune selling 'one-arm bandit' machines and, in 1970, was appointed a director at Easter Road. In time, he would rise to the very top of the game, becoming president of the Scottish Football Association. His death, on January 13, 1984, was a huge loss. As a player, he won 24 Scottish caps.

You, the fan.

HIBERNIAN IN EUROPE

1955/56 - European Cup

1st	Rot Weiss Essen (West Germany)	4-0	A	E Turnbullx2, L Reilly, W Ormond
1st	Rot Weiss Essen	1-1	H	J Buchanan
2nd	Djurgaarden (Sweden)	3-1	A	J Mulkerrin, B Combe, Ake Olsson(og)
2nd	Djurgaarden	1-0	H	E Turnbull (pen)
SF	Stade Reim(France)	0-2	A	(Parc de Princes, Paris) -
SF	Stade Reim	0-1	H	-

1960/61 - Fairs Cup

1st	Lausanne Sports (Switzerland)	'Walkover'		
2nd	Barcelona(Spain)	4-4	A	J Bakerx2, T Preston, J McLeod
2nd	Barcelona	3-2	H	J Baker, T Preston, B Kinloch(pen)
SF	AS Roma(Italy)	2-2	H	J Baker, J McLeod
SF	AS Roma	3-3	A	J Bakerx2, B Kinloch
SF	AS Roma	0-6	A	-

1961/62 - Fairs Cup

1st	Belenenses (Portugal)	3-3	H	J Fraserx2, S Baird (pen)
1st	Belenenses	3-1	A	J Baxterx2, E Stevenson
2nd	Red Star Belgrade (Yugoslavia)	0-4	A	-
2nd	Red Star Belgrade	0-1	H	-

1962/63 - Fairs Cup

1st	Staevnet Copenhagen (Denmark)	4-0	H	M Stevenson, G Byrne, G Baker, Lief Ronnow (og)
1st	Staevnet Copenhagen	3-2	A	M Stevensonx2, G Byrne
2nd	Utrecht(Holland)	2-1	H	G Baker, M Stevenson
2nd	Utrecht	1-0	A	D Falconer
3rd	Valencia(Spain)	0-5	A	-
3rd	Valencia	2-1	H	G Baker, T Preston

1965/66 - Fairs Cup

1st	Valencia(Spain)	2-0	H	J McNamee, J Scott
1st	Valencia	0-2	A	-
1st	Valencia	0-3	A	-

1967/68 - Fairs Cup

1st	Porto(Portugal)	3-0	H	P Cormackx2, E Stevenson
1st	Porto	1-3	A	J Davis(pen)
2nd	Napoli(Italy)	1-4	A	C Stein
2nd	Napoli	5-0	H	B Duncan, P Quinn, P Cormack, P Stanton, C Stein
3rd	Leeds United (England)	0-1	A	-
3rd	Leeds United	1-1	H	C Stein

1968/69 - Fairs Cup

1st	Olympia Ljubljana (Yugoslavia)	3-0	A	E Stevenson, C Stein, Milos Soskic (og)
1st	Olympia Ljubljana	2-1	H	J Davisx2(2 pens)
2nd	Lokomotiv Leipzig (East Germany)	3-1	H	J McBride Snrx3
2nd	Lokomotiv Leipzig	1-0	A	C Grant
3rd	Hamburg (West Germany)	0-1	A	-
3rd	Hamburg	2-1	H	J McBride Snrx2

(lost on the 'away goals' rule)

1970/71 - Fairs Cup

1st	Malmo(Sweden)	6-0	H	J McBride Snrx3, A Duncanx2, J Blair
1st	Malmo	3-2	A	P Stanton, W McEwan, A Duncan
2nd	Vitoria Guimaraes (Portugal)	2-0	H	P Stanton, A Duncan
2nd	Vitoria Guimaraes	1-2	A	J Graham
3rd	Liverpool(England)	0-1	H	-
3rd	Liverpool	0-2	A	-

1972/73 - Cup Winners' Cup

1st	Sporting Lisbon (Portugal)	1-2	A	A Duncan
1st	Sporting Lisbon	6-1	H	A Gordonx2, J O'Rourkex3, Carlos Manaca(og)
2nd	Besa(Albania)	7-1	H	J O'Rourkex3, A Duncanx2, A Cropley, J Brownlie
2nd	Besa	1-1	A	A Gordon
QF	Hajduk Split(Yugoslavia)	4-2	H	A Gordonx3, A Duncan
QF	Hajduk Split	0-3	A	-

1973/74 - UEFA Cup

1st	Keflavik(Iceland)	2-0	H	J Black, T Higgins
1st	Keflavik	1-1	A	P Stanton
2nd	Leeds United	0-0	A	-
2nd	Leeds United	0-0	H	-

(lost on penalties, 4-5)

1974/75 - UEFA Cup

1st	Rosenborg Trondheim (Norway)	3-2	A	P Stanton, A Gordon, A Cropley
1st	Rosenborg Trondheim	9-1	H	J Harperx2, I Munrox2, A Cropleyx 2, P Stantonx2, A Gordon
2nd	Juventus(Italy)	2-4	H	P Stanton, A Cropley
2nd	Juventus	0-4	A	-

1975/76 - UEFA Cup

1st	Liverpool(England)	1-0	H	J Harper
1st	Liverpool	1-3	A	A Edwards

1976/77 - UEFA Cup

1st	Sochaux (France)	1-0	H	J Brownlie
1st	Sochaux	0-0	A	-
2nd	Oesters Vaxjoe (Sweden)	2-0	H	J Blackley, J Brownlie(pen)
2nd	Oesters Vaxjoe	1-4	A	R Smith

1978/79 - UEFA Cup

1st	Norrkoping(Sweden)	3-2	H	T Higginsx2, W Temperley
1st	Norrkoping	0-0	A	-
2nd	Racing Strasbourg (France)	0-2	A	-
2nd	Racing Strasbourg	1-0	H	A McLeod(pen)

1989/90 - UEFA Cup

1st	Videoton(Hungary)	1-0	H	G Mitchell
1st	Videoton	3-0	A	K Houchen, G Evans, J Collins
2nd	FC Liege(Belgium)	0-0	H	-
2nd	FC Liege	0-1 (aet)	A	-

1991/92 - UEFA Cup

1st	Anderlecht(Belgium)	2-2	H	D Beaumont, P McGinlay
1st	Anderlecht	1-1	A	D Jackson

(lost on the 'away goals' rule)

HIBERNIAN – LEAGUE AND CUP PERFORMANCES

Season	Div	P	W	D	L	F	A	Pts	Pos	Scottish Cup	Lgue Cup
1877/78	n/a	n/a	n/a	n/a	n/a	n/a	n/a	n/a	n/a	5th	n/a
1878/79	n/a	n/a	n/a	n/a	n/a	n/a	n/a	n/a	n/a	5th	n/a
1879/80	n/a	n/a	n/a	n/a	n/a	n/a	n/a	n/a	n/a	6th	n/a
1880/81	n/a	n/a	n/a	n/a	n/a	n/a	n/a	n/a	n/a	3rd	n/a
1881/82	n/a	n/a	n/a	n/a	n/a	n/a	n/a	n/a	n/a	5th	n/a
1882/83	n/a	n/a	n/a	n/a	n/a	n/a	n/a	n/a	n/a	5th	n/a
1883/84	n/a	n/a	n/a	n/a	n/a	n/a	n/a	n/a	n/a	SF	n/a
1884/85	n/a	n/a	n/a	n/a	n/a	n/a	n/a	n/a	n/a	SF	n/a
1885/86	n/a	n/a	n/a	n/a	n/a	n/a	n/a	n/a	n/a	SF	n/a
1886/87	n/a	n/a	n/a	n/a	n/a	n/a	n/a	n/a	n/a	W	n/a
1887/88	n/a	n/a	n/a	n/a	n/a	n/a	n/a	n/a	n/a	3rd	n/a
1888/89	n/a	n/a	n/a	n/a	n/a	n/a	n/a	n/a	n/a	1st	n/a
1889/90	n/a	n/a	n/a	n/a	n/a	n/a	n/a	n/a	n/a	6th	n/a
1890/91	dnp	dnp	dnp	dnp	dnp	dnp	dnp	dnp	dnp	2nd	n/a
1891/92	dnp	dnp	dnp	dnp	dnp	dnp	dnp	dnp	dnp	dnp	n/a
1892/93	dnp	dnp	dnp	dnp	dnp	dnp	dnp	dnp	dnp	dnp	n/a
1893/94	2	18	13	3	2	83	29	29	1st	QC	n/a
1894/95	2	18	14	2	2	92	28	30	1st	2nd	n/a
1895/96	1	18	11	2	5	58	39	24	3rd	RU	n/a
1896/97	1	18	12	2	4	50	20	26	2nd	2nd	n/a
1897/98	1	18	10	2	6	47	29	22	3rd	3rd	n/a
1898/99	1	18	10	3	5	42	43	23	4th	2nd	n/a
1899/1900	1	18	9	6	3	43	24	24	3rd	2nd	n/a
1900/01	1	20	9	7	4	29	22	25	3rd	SF	n/a
1901/02	1	18	6	4	8	36	23	16	6th	W	n/a
1902/03	1	22	16	5	1	48	·18	37	1st	3rd	n/a
1903/04	1	26	7	5	14	31	42	19	10	2nd	n/a
1904/05	1	26	9	8	9	39	39	26	5	1st	n/a
1905/06	1	30	10	5	15	35	40	25	11	3rd	n/a
1906/07	1	34	10	10	14	40	49	30	12th	SF	n/a
1907/08	1	34	17	8	9	55	42	42	5th	3rd	n/a
1908/09	1	34	16	7	11	40	32	39	6th	2nd	n/a
1909/10	1	34	14	6	14	33	40	34	8th	SF	n/a
1910/11	1	34	15	6	13	44	48	36	9th	1st	n/a
1911/12	1	34	12	5	17	44	47	29	13th	1st	n/a
1912/13	1	34	16	5	13	63	54	37	8th	3rd	n/a
1913/14	1	38	12	6	20	58	75	30	13th	RU	n/a
1914/15	1	38	12	11	15	59	66	35	11th	n/a	n/a
1915/16	1	38	9	7	22	44	71	25	19th	n/a	n/a
1916/17	1	38	10	10	18	57	72	30	17th	n/a	n/a
1917/18	1	34	8	9	17	42	57	25	16th	n/a	n/a
1918/19	1	34	5	3	26	30	91	13	18th	n/a	n/a
1919/20	1	42	13	7	22	60	79	33	18th	2nd	n/a
1920/21	1	42	16	9	17	58	57	41	13th	2nd	n/a
1921/22	1	42	16	14	12	55	44	46	7th	2nd	n/a
1922/23	1	38	17	7	14	45	40	41	8th	RU	n/a
1923/24	1	38	15	11	12	66	52	41	7th	RU	n/a
1924/25	1	38	22	8	8	78	43	52	3rd	1st	n/a
1925/26	1	38	12	6	20	72	77	30	16th	2nd	n/a

Season	Div	P	W	D	L	F	A	Pts	Pos	Scottish Cup	Lgue Cup
1926/27	1	38	16	7	15	62	71	39	9th	1st	n/a
1927/28	1	38	13	9	16	73	75	35	12th	SF	n/a
1928/29	1	38	13	6	19	54	62	32	14th	1st	n/a
1929/30	1	38	9	11	18	45	62	29	17th	3rd	n/a
1930/31	1	38	9	7	22	49	81	25	19th (R)	3rd	n/a
1931/32	2	38	18	8	12	73	52	44	7th	1st	n/a
1932/33	2	34	25	4	5	80	29	54	1st	4th	n/a
1933/34	1	38	12	3	23	51	69	27	16th	3rd	n/a
1934/35	1	38	14	8	16	59	70	36	11th	3rd	n/a
1935/36	1	38	11	7	20	56	82	29	17th	2nd	n/a
1936/37	1	38	6	13	19	54	83	25	17th	2nd	n/a
1937/38	1	38	11	13	14	57	65	35	10th	1st	n/a
1938/39	1	38	14	7	17	68	69	35	13th	SF	n/a
1939/40	A	5	2	0	3	11	13	4	14th	n/a	n/a

Unofficial league and various cups for the remainder of the Second World War.

Season	Div	P	W	D	L	F	A	Pts	Pos	Scottish Cup	Lgue Cup
1945/46	A	30	17	6	7	67	37	40	2nd	n/a	n/a
1946/47	A	30	19	6	5	69	33	44	2nd	RU	SF
1947/48	A	30	22	4	4	86	27	48	1st	SF	QS
1948/49	A	30	17	5	8	75	52	39	3rd	4th	QS
1949/50	A	30	22	5	3	86	34	49	2nd	1st	SF
1950/51	A	30	22	4	4	78	26	48	1st	SF	RU
1951/52	A	30	20	5	5	92	36	45	1st	1st	QS
1952/53	A	30	19	5	6	93	51	43	2nd	4th	SF
1953/54	A	30	15	4	11	72	51	34	5th	3rd	SF
1954/55	A	30	15	4	11	64	54	34	5th	5th	QS
1955/56	A	34	19	7	8	86	50	45	4th	5th	QS
1956/57	1	34	12	9	13	69	56	33	9th	5th	QS
1957/58	1	34	13	5	16	59	60	31	9th	RU	QS
1958/59	1	34	13	6	15	68	70	32	10th	4th	QS
1959/60	1	34	14	7	13	106	85	35	7th	4th	QS
1960/61	1	34	15	4	15	66	69	34	8th	4th	QS
1961/62	1	34	14	5	15	58	72	33	8th	1st	QS
1962/63	1	34	8	9	17	47	67	25	16th	3rd	QS
1963/64	1	34	12	6	16	59	66	30	10th	1st	SF
1964/65	1	34	21	4	9	75	47	46	4th	SF	QS
1965/66	1	34	16	6	12	81	55	38	6th	2nd	SF
1966/67	1	34	19	4	11	72	49	42	5th	3rd	QS
1967/68	1	34	20	5	9	67	49	45	3rd	2nd	QS
1968/69	1	34	12	7	15	60	59	31	12th	1st	RU
1969/70	1	34	19	6	9	65	40	44	3rd	1st	QS
1970/71	1	34	10	10	14	47	53	30	12th	SF	QF
1971/72	1	34	19	6	9	62	34	44	4th	RU	QF
1972/73	1	34	19	7	8	74	33	45	3rd	4th	W
1973/74	1	34	20	9	5	75	42	49	2nd	5th	2nd
1974/75	1	34	20	9	5	69	37	49	2nd	3rd	RU
1975/76	P	36	18	7	11	55	43	43	3rd	5th	QF
1976/77	P	36	8	18	10	34	35	34	6th	4th	QS
1977/78	P	36	15	7	14	51	43	37	4th	4th	1st
1978/79	P	36	12	13	11	44	48	37	5th	RU*	SF
1979/80	P	36	6	6	24	29	67	18	10(R)	SF	3rd
1980/81	F	39	24	9	6	67	24	57	1st	5th	4th

Season	Div	P	W	D	L	F	A	Pts	Pos	Scottish Cup	Lgue Cup
1981/82	P	36	11	14	11	38	40	36	6th	4th	QS
1982/83	P	36	7	15	14	35	51	29	7th	3rd	QS
1983/84	P	36	12	7	17	45	55	31	7th	3rd	3rd
1984/85	P	36	10	7	19	38	61	27	8th	3rd	3rd
1985/86	P	36	11	6	19	49	63	28	8th	SF	RU
1986/87	P	44	10	13	21	44	70	33	9th	4th	4th
1987/88	P	44	12	19	13	41	42	43	6th	4th	4th
1988/89	P	36	13	9	14	37	36	35	5th	SF	4th
1989/90	P	36	12	10	14	32	41	34	7th	5th	4th
1990/91	P	36	6	13	17	24	51	25	9th	4th	3rd
1991/92	P	44	16	17	11	53	45	49	5th	5th	Winners
1992/93	P	44	12	13	19	54	64	37	7th	SF	3rd
1993/94	P	44	16	15	13	53	48	47	5th	4th	RU
1994/95	P	36	12	17	7	49	37	53	3rd	SF	4th
1995/96	P	36	11	10	15	43	57	43	5th	3rd	3rd
1996/97	P	36	9	11	16	38	55	38	9th+	4th	4th
1997/98	P	36	6	12	18	38	59	30	10(R)	3rd	3rd

n/a - Not applicable
dnp - Did not participate
QC - Qualifying Cup
QS - Qualifying Section
RU - Runners up
W - Winners
R - Relegated
P - Premier Division
A - 'A' Division
1 - Division One
2 - Division Two

* Lost second replay of Cup Final. First game - May 12, 1979 - Hibernian 0 Rangers 0. Second game - May 16, 1979 - Hibernian 0 Rangers 0. Third game - May 28, 1979 - Hibernian 2 (Higgins, MacLeod, pen) Rangers 3 (Johnstone x2, Duncan og). All games played at Hampden Park.

+ Remained in Premier Division after play-off versus Airdrie:

First leg, Saturday, May 17, 1997 Hibernian 1 (Cooper og 13) Airdrie 0.

Second leg, Thursday May 22, 1997 Airdrie 2 (Connolly 2, Black 88, pen) Hibernian 4 (Jackson D 46 pen, 70 pen, Tosh 73, Wright 83).

Hibernian won 5-2 on aggregate.

LEAGUE CUP FINALS

October 28, 1950 Motherwell 3 Hibernian 0 Team: T Younger, J Govan, J Ogilvie, A Buchanan, J Paterson, B Combe, G Smith, B Johnstone, L Reilly, W Ormond, J Bradley. Played at Hampden Park.

April 5, 1969 Celtic 6 Hibernian 2 (O'Rourke, E Stevenson) Team: T Allan, A Shevlane, J Davis, P Stanton, J Madsen, J Blackley, P Marinello, P Quinn, P Cormack, J O'Rourke, E Stevenson. Played at Hampden Park.

December 9, 1972 Hibernian 2 (Stanton, O'Rourke) Celtic 1 Team: J Herriot, J Brownlie, E Schaedler, P Stanton, J Black, J Blackley, A Edwards, J O'Rourke, A Gordon, A Cropley, A Duncan. Played at Hampden Park.

October 26, 1974 Celtic 6 Hibernian 3 (Harper x3) Team: J McArthur, J Brownlie (R Smith), D Bremner, P Stanton, D Spalding, J Blackley, A Edwards, A Cropley, J Harper, I Munro, A Duncan (W Murray). Played at Hampden Park.

October 27, 1985 Aberdeen 3 Hibernian 0 Team: A Rough, A Sneddon, I Munro, A Brazil (C Harris), M Fulton, G Hunter, P Kane, G Chisholm, S Cowan, G Durie, J McBride (J Collins). Played at Hampden Park.

October 27, 1991 Hibernian 2 (McIntyre(pen), Wright) Dunfermline 1 Team: J Burridge, W Miller, G Mitchell, G Hunter, T McIntyre, M MacLeod, M Weir, B Hamilton, K Wright, G Evans, P McGinlay. Played at Hampden Park.

October 24, 1993 Rangers 2 Hibernian 1 (McPherson(og)) Team: J Leighton, W Miller, G Mitchell, D Farrell, S Tweed, G Hunter, K McAllister, B Hamilton, K Wright, D Jackson (G Evans), M O'Neill. Played at Celtic Park.

TOP GOALSCORERS SINCE THE START OF THE PREMIER DIVISION*

1975/76 Arthur Duncan 13

1976/77 Bobby Smith 8

1977/78 Ally MacLeod 16

1978/79 Ralph Callaghan 9

1979/80 Ally MacLeod 8

1980/81 Ally MacLeod 15+

1981/82 Gordon Rae 11

1982/83 Gary Murray/Gordon Rae/Bobby Thomson 6

1983/84 Willie Irvine 18

1984/85 Gordon Durie/Paul Kane 8

1985/86 Stevie Cowan 19

1986/87 George McCluskey 9

1987/88 Paul Kane 10

1988/89 Steve Archibald 13

1989/90 Keith Houchen 8

1990/91 Paul Wright 6

1991/92 Mickey Weir 11

1992/93 Darren Jackson 13

1993/94 Keith Wright 16

1994/95 Darren Jackson/Michael O'Neill/Keith Wright 10

1995/96 Darren Jackson/Keith Wright 9

1996/97 Darren Jackson 11

1997/98 Steve Crawford 9

* League goals only

+ All in Premier Division, except in 1980/81: First Division

FACTFILE

Hibernian FC, Founded: 1875

Honours & Records:

Scottish League winners (4): 1902/03, 1947/48, 1950/51, 1951/52

First Division winners (1): 1980/81

Division Two winners (3): 1893/94, 1894/85, 1932/33

Division One runners-up (6): 1896/97, 1946/47, 1949/50, 1952/53, 1973/74, 1974/75

Scottish Cup winners (2): 1887, 1902

Scottish Cup runners-up (8): 1896, 1914, 1923, 1924, 1947, 1958, 1972, 1979

Scottish League Cup winners (2): 1972/73, 1991/92

Scottish League Cup runners-up (5): 1950/51, 1968/69, 1974/75, 1985/86, 1993/94

Drybrough Cup winners (2): 1972/73, 1973/74

Summer Cup winners (2): 1941, 1964

Tennents Sixes winners (1): 1989/90

BP Youth Cup winners (1): 1991/92

European Cup: six matches (best: semi final 1955/56)

Cup Winners' Cup: six matches (best: third round 1972/73)

UEFA/Fairs Cup: 60 matches (best: semi final Fairs Cup 1960/61)

Record home attendance: 65,860 versus Heart of Midlothian, January 2 1950

Most capped player: Lawrie Reilly, 38, Scotland

Most league appearances: Arthur Duncan, 446

Most league goals in a season by an individual: Joe Baker, 42, 1959/60 season

Most goals by an individual (all seasons): Gordon Smith, 364

Record victory (all matches): 22-1 versus 42nd Highlanders, September 3, 1881

Record victory (league only): (record 'home' league win) 11-1 versus Hamilton Academical, November 6, 1965; (record 'away' league win) 11-1 versus Airdrie, October 24, 1959.

Record victory (Premier Division only): 8-1 versus Kilmarnock April 2, 1983

Record victory (Scottish Cup only): 15-1 versus Peebles Rovers, February 11, 1961

Record victory (League Cup): 11-2 versus Alloa, September 22, 1965

Record victory (Europe): 9-1 versus Rosenborg Trondheim, UEFA Cup, October 2, 1974

Record defeat (all matches): 0-10 versus Rangers, December 24, 1898

Record defeat (league only): 0-10 versus Rangers, December 24, 1898

Record defeat (Premier Division only): 0-7 versus Rangers, December 30, 1995

Record defeat (Scottish Cup only): 1-9 versus Dumbarton, September 27, 1890

Record defeat (League Cup): 1-6 versus Hearts, August 11, 1956, and Rangers, August 8, 1958

Record defeat (Europe): 0-6 versus Roma, Fairs Cup, May 27, 1961

Address: Easter Road Stadium, Edinburgh EH7 5QG

Telephone Nos: Switchboard 0131-661 2159

Ticket Hotline and Club Shop: 0131-661 1875

Forthview Restaurant: 0131-661 3618

Internet: www.hibs.co.uk